THE B.

WHAT THEY HAVE WRITTEN ABOUT THE BORO FIRM

"After Man United, I rate them the best." Andy Nicholls, *Scally*

"If you went by ordinary train you'd have to be mob-handed, because Boro was simply the worst ground in the league, apart from Liverpool, for getting sussed and having your trainees or sovereign rings robbed." Nicky Allt, *The Boys From The Mersey*

"They still have a good firm now." Mickey Francis, *Guvnors*

"Boro don't mess about . . . the best firm I had seen come to Cardiff." Tony Rivers, *Soul Crew*

"They must put something in the babies' milk up there . . . pound for pound they're very good and they will have a proper go." Rob Silvester, *Rolling With The 6.57 Crew*

THE BRICK

A Hooligan's Story

Paul Debrick

MILO BOOKS

Published in paperback in September 2005 by Milo Books

Copyright © 2005 Paul Debrick

ISBN 1 903854 47 4

Typeset by Avon DataSet Ltd,
Bidford on Avon, Warwickshire, B50 4JH

Printed and bound in Great Britain by
Creative Print and Design, Ebbw Vale, Gwent

MILO BOOKS LTD
The Old Weighbridge
Station Road
Wrea Green
Lancs PR4 2PH
info@milobooks.com

CONTENTS

DEDICATION

I dedicate this book to my son, Tommy.

Tommy, you bring a smile to my face each and every day. You have brought so much happiness into my life and for that I will try to guide you and teach you right from wrong.

In my past I have had a lot of good times and a lot of bad so, with my experience I will try to bring you up to be a good person.

I am looking forward to watching you grow and I see that you have already got your own little personality and a proper little sense of humour, so I know we will share some very funny and happy times together.

You are my little ray of sunshine and I love you so much.

INTRODUCTION

I know what you're thinking: *not another football hooligan book.* Well it is, partly. On the other hand, it's different.

When people write football hooligan books, they're all about my beloved Everton, my brilliant Chelsea, marvellous Middlesbrough and so on. Personally, I couldn't give two fucks about Middlesbrough Football Club, never have, never will.

The truth is I used Middlesbrough as an excuse to vent my violence on anyone we played. Why? Because I love a bit of violence, and football was as good an excuse as any. I can honestly say in my twenty-odd years of travelling with the Boro 'Casual Firm', at any one given time I couldn't name the team. It took me two years to learn the offside rule, but who gives a fuck?

So in this book you won't find results, attendances or goal scorers, because in all honesty I don't know them myself. What you will find is my account of my time running with the mob, from the beginning to ultimately being 'top boy', going to jail, working the doors and a few other bits thrown in.

In football circles most people know me as 'The Brick', some know me as Debrick and some even know me as that big, good-looking fucker. Well it is my book and, yes, I'm probably biased but I'll write what I want. I know I will get slagged by some of you

1

for not being a genuine football fan and I will probably get a ban thrown in for good measure, but I have got thick skin, so bring it on. I hope you enjoy reading this as much as I enjoyed writing it.

* * *

Our mob is called the Frontline. While I was writing this book, people from all over the place asked me when was the Frontline started and how was it formed. It started in the very early Eighties. Hooliganism had kicked off big time and mobs were running amok on a Saturday afternoon all over the country. It was the heyday of West Ham's notorious Inter City Firm, Chelsea's Headhunters, and the Arsenal Gooners, to name but a few. Most clubs at that time were just getting organised and finding their feet.

Middlesbrough's mob didn't have a name. We were just a set of lads who loved an 'off' and were just getting it together as far as the casual scene went. Somebody came up with the name "Frontline" one day and, before anyone realised, it stuck.

We quickly became an established and organised firm and soon had a reputation throughout the country as a top mob. This reputation has stayed with us for over two decades and we didn't get it by beating up scarf heads or smashing things up. Our reputation was built on being game. Even when we were well outnumbered, we were still there doing it. We were from a small town in the North East of England but we built a reputation against all the major cities throughout the country. Any club that has come up against us will know I'm not blowing my own trumpet and that I speak the truth. There's only a handful of clubs to this day that have ever come into Middlesbrough early on match days and gone looking for it.

Frontline is not a name that we used as a banner. Like I said, it just stuck with us throughout the years. The name Frontline didn't really matter to the lads I travelled with, you could have called us anything. What was important to us was turning over different mobs, regardless of whether we had a name or not. So people who come up with "it started like this or that" and post it on the websites, get a life. I've told you how it started. I should know, I was there.

HEMLINGTON

I WAS BROUGHT UP by my mother and father with my older brother, Mark, in the rough part of a council estate in Hemlington. My father worked as a painter and decorator and, although he liked his drink and gambling, he was kept on the straight and narrow by my mother, who was a cook at Middlesbrough Fire Station. Although in my early days I was never exposed to violence I was soon to learn what it was all about.

Hemlington is a sprawl of housing just south of Middlesbrough, made up of several different estates that merged together. The houses were cheaply-built, some pebble-dashed, some three-storey, but mainly two-up, two-downs. At the bottom end of Hemlington were some private houses and if you lived there you were called "posh". Our family couldn't afford to live there so we had make do with a two-up, two-down. There was a shopping complex in the middle of the estate where youths congregated at night and generally did what kids do all over the country: smoke, drink and cause a nuisance.

My first taste of theft was on our weekly shopping trip to a well-known supermarket every Thursday night. Once we were in the store, my father would tell my brother and I to eat what we wanted. We walked around, grabbing different items off the shelves and stuffing our faces. We didn't know we were doing anything wrong. Many is the time we left the supermarket fit to burst. We loved our dad because we thought we were getting a treat off him, though he was actually teaching us how to shoplift.

I attended Viewley Hill Primary School, which was pretty uneventful, but that changed when I went to secondary school. My first real taste of violence came at the Protestant Hustler Secondary School in Acklam. It was right next to St George's Catholic School, a sure recipe for trouble. One morning, on my way to school, I saw a group of lads from my school waiting to ambush some Catholics. Soon enough, three or four of them came walking down the path. What happened next was incredible. Out of the blue, the lads from my school ran up and laid into these others. They were lambs to the slaughter. Each and every one was beaten to a pulp and had to run for their lives, with blood pouring from their noses and mouths.

I wasn't scared or anything like that. In fact I got a massive buzz out of it. I thought to myself that I wouldn't mind a bit of that more often. When I walked down the same path the next morning, the same lads from my school were there and I thought, here's MY chance. I waited with them for about five minutes until, inevitably, along came our victims. They were older than me and slightly bigger but I thought, fuck it, and ran straight at them. The other lads with me followed and, just like the day before, four Catholics got a kicking. The feeling of power was overwhelming. I'd tasted violence first hand and, if violence was a drug, I was hooked there and then.

It wasn't a religious thing, with them being Catholics and us being Protestants. They could have been Chinese or Pakistanis, anything, we didn't care. It was simply "us against them", whoever they might be. We walked to school that morning proud as punch and all the other lads congratulated me for being "game as fuck". Brilliant, I thought, I'd joined my first gang.

We continued our onslaught on our rival school for a couple of years until I moved to a school closer to my home, Coulby Newham Secondary. A trip to Billingham Forum ice rink was organised and we went skating. As we came out, a coachload of kids from a school in Stockton were waiting to go in to skate. One of them made a skitty remark, so I whacked him on the jaw and he hit the deck like a bust lift. This signalled the other lads on our bus to go "Beirut" and the skitty twats all got a good kicking.

Back at school, I was hauled before the headmaster and promptly suspended. Like I gave a fuck! I hated school and left in April, 1981, aged sixteen and without a single qualification. I couldn't get a job in Middlesbrough, which at the time was plagued by very high unemployment, so I went in search of work with my brother, Mark, and two other lads to the bright lights of Blackpool. We shared a flat in Dickson Road, found jobs glass collecting in a nightclub and had a whale of a time.

The nightclub was called the Touchdown Tavern and was next to Blackpool bus station on Talbot Road. You paid in and walked down a steep flight of stairs to get to the club, which was in the basement, dark and dingy, with a small dancefloor on the right as you entered and a long bar on the left. They had cheap promotion nights throughout the week – £10 in but a penny a pint, that kind of thing – all through the week, so it was busy all the time, mostly with holidaymakers, many of them Jocks. As glass collectors, we quickly got to know the doormen at the club. They were a pretty tough crew who loved a good battle, and they actually told us to start fights so that they could get stuck into the punters. It was their idea of a good time. So every single night we'd walk up to groups of lads and, whack, cop that you fucker, always safe in the knowledge that we had a team of doormen behind us. And with only one way in and out, if the doormen collared you there was no way out without a good kicking. This went on right through the summer season and, by the end, I was pretty good at this violence thing. In fact I thrived on it.

My mother, Linda, had been suffering with cervical cancer for some time and, sadly, she died the day after I returned home. She was only forty-two, which I'm sure you will agree is no age to die. She was a hardworking woman who wanted the best for her two boys, and her death was a body blow to me. I was devastated. I knew my dad, Ronny, would go off the rails without my mam. He did, and as I had predicted, we ended up in a small, two-bedroom council flat after he failed to pay the mortgage.

My mother had been the steadying factor in the family and I knew the whole thing would go pear-shaped when she died. I honestly believe that was a turning point in my life, when I went off the rails. When she was alive I was no angel, but without her I went from bad to worse. With no-one to teach me right from wrong, I just did my own thing. People say I am easily influenced by the wrong things in life, and the paths and people that I chose at this time were probably wrong. But as they say, shit happens – and I was soon to end in deep shit. I often wonder how I would have turned out had my mam lived, but I will never know.

My dad was the other side of the coin, so to speak. He was a drinker and a gambler and couldn't give a shit what Mark and I did. I can remember him saying to me, from an early age, "If you're going to rob something, make sure you don't get caught, and if you do get caught then deny it." In my eyes now that's pretty sound advice, but when you're young and you hear your old fella saying that, you think you've got the right to go and take whatever you want – which I did.

In hindsight, I can't believe my mother and father stayed together as long as they did. Many's the time he came home on a

Thursday or Friday night having lost all his wages in the bookie's. There was hell on in our house every weekend. Often his Sunday dinner would be on the table and my old fella wouldn't show, preferring to stay in the club with his mates and get pissed. In short he was a waster. Not that he was all bad – he did teach me how to shoplift!

I started going to Northern Soul all-nighters at Rotherham and Cleethorpes and turned to speed and barbiturates in a big way. Anyone who knows me will tell you I can't do things normally or by halves, I have to take everything to its limit and this was no exception. It was at these all-nighters we met lads from Hull: Enoch, Greg Carroll (R.I.P.), Arthur Sean, Nelly Platton, Pete Webster and Mike Lamoty, to name but a few. They were all into football violence and we got to know them all quite well and had several days out in Hull and at Boothferry Park. The all-nighters eventually shut down and we lost touch with each other. Later, however, that friendship helped us at a friendly match at Hull City that you'll read about in another chapter.

JUNIOR HOOLIGAN

IT WAS BY chance that I stumbled over my first real taste of football violence. Unbeknown to me, it was going to change my Saturday afternoons and my life. I was in Middlesbrough one Saturday when the team was playing at home at Ayresome Park against our arch rivals, Newcastle United. We walked around the town centre for some time and then one of my mates suggested that we walk up to the Linthorpe pub for a drink, then on to the ground to see what was going on. We set off up Linthorpe Road to get to the pub and, while we were walking, I noticed lads hanging about all over the place. As anybody knows, when you play a derby match, especially against somebody like Newcastle, there is always trouble and this day was going to be no exception.

We arrived at the pub and bought a drink. It was packed with lads and everybody was talking about what was going to happen that afternoon. Everybody was saying that it was going to go off, big time, so there was a general buzz about the place. I was no stranger to a bit of violence by then so I decided that I would have a couple of pints and then go down to Ayresome Park to see what was happening. I didn't really understand what football violence was all about, but that was about to change.

Five of us left the pub and walked towards Ayresome Park, only half a mile away, along Linthorpe Road, the main road which runs from the train station into the town centre and right past the old ground. Away fans had to walk along it in order to get to the game. Once at the top of Linthorpe Road, you had to negotiate side streets lined with terraced houses. It didn't matter which way you came to Ayresome Park, you always had to walk down these streets, as the ground was surrounded by them. It was like a maze if you weren't familiar with them, brilliant for ambushes, as I would find out.

At the ground people were milling around all over the place. We walked around to the old 'Bob' End section and stood there waiting to see what was going to happen; we didn't have to wait long. We were just sitting on the wall when I noticed a large gang of lads coming round the corner. They looked different to any other football fans I had seen before. They didn't have scarves on or colours of any description to associate them with Middlesbrough Football Club. I wasn't sure who they were at the time. One of the lads I was sat with said, "They are the NTP." N, T and P were the initials of three council estates in Middlesbrough - Netherfields, Thorntree and Park End. Lads from these estates had merged and now formed a formidable force wherever they went. This gang looked quite organised as they all walked together. No one was singing, shouting or making a nuisance, they just walked in an orderly fashion as if they were some kind of regiment. They all had wedged haircuts and were dressed similarly in faded jeans, white trainers and smart jumpers.

I wondered where they were going as they turned left into Kensington Road and started to walk away from the ground. I decided to follow with one of my friends. "They must know where some Geordies are and are on their way to front them," said my mate. I kept a short distance behind them and as we approached Linthorpe Road, sure enough, from around the corner came thirty

Geordies. There must have been around the same number of NTP lads and I heard them say, "Here they are, keep it tight," and, "Wait until they get really close." I knew an attack was inevitable so I moved closer.

When the Geordies realised what was happening it was too late. The NTP charged at the same time, they were like a swarm of wasps. "Come on, you Geordie bastards," someone shouted and the NTP lads attacked them at the side of the road. They were laid out left, right and centre. I saw a fat Geordie on the floor, getting kicked senseless. It brought memories of my schooldays flooding back, only this was on a much bigger scale. As I said earlier, Ayresome Park was like a rat run with all the side streets around it and these Geordies had nowhere to go, they were just getting picked off. The few that did manage to get away and run down the street had kicks and punches aimed at them by just about anybody. I knew that Newcastle and Middlesbrough didn't like each other but this was real hate.

The NTP lads moved on and walked down another side street running adjacent to the ground. I was buzzing with what I'd just witnessed and I wasn't going to miss more of the same. The police presence in those days was minimal, even on derby days, unlike today. You could get away with murder. Now you can't even fart at a game without being nicked. As you probably know, these days you're tracked from the minute you leave your home town by spotters, CCTV, helicopters, you name it they use it. The odds are now stacked against the would-be football hooligan, and I don't think it will ever again be like it was in those early days.

As the NTP approached another side street, fifteen lads were getting off a minibus that had just parked up. "Here's some more," I heard the lads say and, sure enough, the bus was attacked, only this time I joined in. As before, the Geordies got a pounding and some even dived back into the bus to take cover, but they were dragged back out on to the road and savagely beaten. I heard a police siren coming along the road and the NTP just stopped what they were doing and casually walked away. Fucking mental, I thought, and from that day on I knew I wanted to be just like them.

We paid into the Bob End terrace and watched the game. All the way through the match, people were screaming abuse at the Geordies and they were doing the same back. You could smell the hatred in the air; it was a very strange atmosphere, one that I wasn't used to. But, even so, I was enjoying myself, watching people being ejected from every part of the ground.

I looked across the pitch at the Holgate End and, all of a sudden the crowd opened up. About thirty Geordies had infiltrated the terrace. The Holgate in those days was a well-known stand and our 'Kop' end, if you like, a place where all the skinheads and lunatics went. Fists were flying in every direction and the crowd seemed to be moving backwards and forwards as the opposing fans fought each other. The whole football ground was going mental and everybody was screaming and shouting. It took a few minutes for the police to restore order, then they took the Geordies out on to the pitch side and marched them round to the away enclosure. The Boro fans were going mad, shouting and screaming abuse, throwing coins, pies and anything that came to hand, but at the other end all the Geordies were cheering these lads on. In their eyes they were heroes.

When we left the ground I quickly followed the NTP lads and watched a mass brawl break out. Hundreds of Geordies had come out of the away end and there was a toe-to-toe battle on the street right outside the ground. The Boro fans had been taken by surprise and were backing off. Some were getting picked off and I could see people getting kicked all over. Suddenly, the whole street seemed to turn back and, with a mighty roar ran straight back into the

Geordies. It was like the fight scene at the beginning of *Gladiator*. It was the Geordies turn to run now and they were on their toes. They turned on their heels but there was nowhere to go. The police were running all over, nicking people, and it took quite some time for them to get between the two rivals gangs and restore order. I continued on towards Linthorpe Road, where fighting was going on everywhere.

Those derby days were amazing, especially at Ayresome Park. I didn't know any of the NTP lads then but I was soon to become a good friend of theirs. What I didn't know at the time was that I would soon be travelling all over the country with these lads, doing the "biz" everywhere and, in later years actually leading them and, eventually, being top boy.

Being into Northern Soul in those days, we'd go to the Beechwood Youth Club, a hangout for the NTP, so I got to know some of them pretty well. A year or so later we moved house to a three-bedroomed house in Coulby Newham, our first real private house and a proper nice place. I thought I was a right posh cunt when we moved in. Mind you, we soon lowered the tone in the road, with police coming to the door and later on having all-night parties with loads of lasses coming back.

I started seeing a girl, and it turned out her older sister was living with one of the NTP top lads who also lived in Coulby Newham. He was called Mickey and we became good friends. Mickey was a real nutcase in his heyday. He had one of these don't-give-a-fuck attitudes, a bit like myself, so we hit it off straight away. Mickey was one of the original casuals or "joeys", as we called them then, and I have some good memories of him over the years. Some of the things we got up to were unreal and Mickey had a proper sense of humour.

One night I was walking my then girlfriend to the bus stop when Mickey got off another bus on the other side of the road.

There were two lads with him and Mickey shouted me over the road. He had a bust nose and I asked him what was wrong. He explained to me that he had been fighting on the bus with these two lads but he was taking them home for a coffee. He then winked at me and asked me if I was coming back with them for a coffee. I said yes because I knew what was going to happen, Mickey being Mickey. I left the girl at the bus stop and walked the short distance to Mickey's upstairs flat, just around the corner. We walked up the stairs into the hallway and Mickey immediately right-handed one of them. The lad ran down the stairs to try to escape but it was too late, Mickey had locked the door. Unlucky, lads. This time, unlike on the bus, there were two of us and two of them. I immediately grabbed the other lad and threw him down the stairs. They were screaming and obviously shitting themselves at what was going to happen. Both got a good kicking and I bet from then on they sat on a bus and stayed quiet.

When we had a home game, some of the NTP lads would go to a well known ski shop in the town centre and turn up at the match in freshly-robbed ski coats. The lads looked really smart in the brightly-coloured clobber. Mickey must have had one in every colour, probably the best collection in the country. You have got to keep warm when you are waiting on the corner for the away fans in the middle of winter.

We played West Ham, a well-known firm at the time, probably the best. The ICF, or Inter-City Firm, were notorious hooligans who travelled the length and breadth of the country, turning everybody over. So when Saturday came, everybody expected a massive mob to come off the train, and people were milling about all over the place. All our lads were drinking in the Masham pub in the town centre. The lads used to drink there because it was in the precinct of Linthorpe Road and you had to walk past it to get to the ground if you were coming from the train station. The ICF didn't disappoint us. Around about 12.30 they came bouncing out of the station into the shopping precinct towards the Masham. A large black lad seemed to be leading them and they seemed very organised. Seventy or eighty of them were walking in a tight knit group and they looked well up for it.

Several police were with them and they just marched straight past the Masham with their police escort and on to Linthorpe Road. They were escorted to the ground with all our lads following on the other side of the road. We weren't as organised as West Ham in those days but we would have given them a run for their money all the same. Once at the ground the ICF went straight into the Middlesbrough seats behind the goal and all our lads were in the adjacent Bob End. There was no real trouble during the game, but when the final whistle went, cool as cucumbers, they stood up together and walked straight over to the fence separating us.

"Do you want it outside?" the black lad boomed.

Game as fuck, I thought. We weren't used to this but we accepted his invitation all the same. Once outside the police got them in a tight escort and marched them back on to Linthorpe Road in order to get them back to the station. We all followed and their mob was showered with just about anything we could find. We came out of every side street all the way back down Linthorpe Road, and bricks, bottles, you name it, we threw it. Shop windows went in, it was like World War III. Give West Ham their due, they were well up for it but they couldn't seem to break the tight police escort surrounding them. As other people have said before, we only fought at matches with like-minded lads who were there for the same thing and were up for it. As any football hooligan knows, nobody smacks a scarf-head, not unless you're from Leeds anyway.

Those very early days were brilliant and we had rucks

everywhere we went. In the early Eighties every mob in the country thought they had something to prove and hooliganism was rife in every major town and city. Football violence got a lot of bad publicity, especially after the Heysel Stadium disaster where thirty-nine people died. That game also cost me my parole, but I will tell you about that in another chapter.

HULL CITY

FOR YEARS I had been doing the Northern Soul circuit with a lot of the lads, going to the all-nighters. I was a pretty nifty dancer back then; mind you, most people were full of speed. It was here we got to know lads from Hull, Sheffield United and Bradford. The Hull lads reckoned they were the best mob in their division and, as luck would have it, or unlucky for them, we were brought together for a pre-season friendly, played at Hull on August 15, 1983.

We had a few weeks to organise ourselves and to sort out transport. We all knew this was a biggy, so much so that if we hadn't got transport we would have probably walked there. We tried all the coach companies but they all fucked us off, apart from the Ellerman Bee Line company, who agreed to take 112 lads to a "twenty-first birthday party". The silly cunts must have thought it was going to be one hell of a party. And so it was, though more than twenty years later, I still don't know whose birthday it was.

The lads turned up on the day and, funnily enough, not one of them had a birthday card. All the nutters were on one bus and the rest on the other. We set off, and what a buzz! Everyone was up for it and we knew we had something to prove.

THE BRICK

The two buses got split up, probably because ours stopped to rob every shop that was open on the way. Unfortunately, some daft twat who had missed the coach went to the Ellerman Bee Line depot and asked what time the two match buses had left for Hull. Our coach was intercepted by the police in Beverley, just outside Hull, and the driver was told to return to Middlesbrough. To our amazement, the police then fucked off and left the poor man on the bus with fifty-five lunatics. He was promptly threatened, and drove on to Hull. This minor set back meant we missed the kick-off, but not the "kick-off" we were looking for.

Some of us had been to Boothferry Park before with the Hull lads, so we knew exactly where they would be in the ground. At about fifteen minutes after kick-off the Hull lads must have thought they were in for a quiet night. How wrong they were.

We ran to the entrance to the West Stand seats without a copper in sight, what a sweet feeling and such a buzz of adrenalin. No drug gives you a buzz like that (though there are a few that come close).

We walked up to the turnstiles and someone threatened the steward with a knife while we all jumped over. You know when you're trying to sleep at night and counting sheep over a gate, one after the other, well that's what it was like. Except these sheep wore Lacoste tracksuits and were fucking mental. When the whole flock was safely over the gate, we congregated in the concourse, ready. We knew that when we got up the stairs, into their seats, their mob would be in a standing section in front of us. We steamed up the stairs and, sure enough, there was the Hull mob minding their own business, cheering on their team. They were like rabbits dazzled in a car's headlights, and we were in the driving seat. Over the wall we went, straight at them. They absolutely shit themselves and ran on to the pitch, swiftly followed by us. We fought on the pitch with the few lads from their mob who actually stood. The element of surprise is always a good thing and, if done correctly, works every time.

The other coachload of lads had arrived before us and was in the away supporters' end. They took their cue from us and ran onto the pitch to make a beeline (sorry, coach company) for the Hull mob. It went off big time in the middle of the pitch and the police just didn't have the manpower to do jack shit. It went off for ages and the Hull lads did a runner for their Main Stand. When order was restored we went back to our stand and watched what was left of the match.

At the end of the game the Hull chairman came on to the pitch to announce that our coaches had returned to Boro without us and that we were stranded. Like we gave a fuck; we knew we'd get another opportunity in the city centre later on. But we were wrong. When we left the ground the police were mob-handed and marched us down to the train station, only to find out the last train had gone. In their wisdom they contacted Middlesbrough FC and asked them to pay for two coaches to return us all to Boro. I'm sure I can still hear the person who answered that phone call at Middlesbrough laughing.

But, to the police's delight and our dismay, the Hull chairman said he would lay on coaches for us and Hull City would foot the bill. It must have been midnight when three vintage double decker buses pulled up. What a sight. I expected Blakey from *On The Buses* to be the conductor. We arrived back in the Boro at three in the morning, to be met by Middlesbrough police. They welcomed us home by setting the dogs on us. The following day we hit the headlines big time.

HUDDERSFIELD

DURING THE 1983 season, football hooliganism was rife. These were the good old days. We played Huddersfield at their ground and took a large mob down. We were all young lads, game and ready for anything. Around seventy of us travelled by train and, as usual, spirits were high. One thing was inevitable; there would be trouble, there always was. Let's face it, it's why we went. Without trouble there would be no point in going.

We emerged from the train station at around 11am and I don't think Huddersfield expected us so early. We would surprise a lot of mobs up and down the country over the years by being early. We quickly found a boozer and were having a few drinks when one of Huddersfield's lads came in and told us his mob were in the Blue Bell pub a bit further into town. We asked directions and set off. No police were around so we knew that, if they were there, we would storm their pub and take it over. Everyone was buzzing at what was about to take place. We weren't really organised in these early days, but we all had one thought in common – trouble. Nowadays, you get a lot of hangers on who turn up fully Stone Islanded up. They look the part but half of them couldn't fill in a sick note. Not in those early days. Everyone who travelled knew everyone else, so everybody stood by one another, no matter what.

THE BRICK

We crossed the precinct and came to an alleyway on the right. Their main pub was just on the other side of the alleyway, and out they came, shouting and bouncing about. We flew straight at them, people were getting whacked all over the place and there wasn't a copper in sight. I was carrying one of those telescopic brollies that hooligans used to carry in the early Eighties, going hammer and tongs with it. The fighting went on for quite some time and we backed them through the alleyway and onto the road. I noticed a fat lad wearing glasses in front of me, and "Whack", he tasted the brolly. As he staggered back he stumbled and slipped on to his fat arse. I immediately tried to re-arrange his head with the brolly and was stood over him going mental when I noticed our lads starting to back off. *What the fuck's going on here?* Then I realised that at the end of the alleyway, no more than fifty yards away, was the police station. And here's us going off big time right under their noses.

As I looked towards the end of the alley I saw thirty or forty coppers running towards us. Picture the scene, forty Keystone Cops running through the alley at us, and me standing over the top of Billy Bunter with my arm going like a piston and a brolly in my hand. You guessed it, locked up straight away. Talk about getting caught in the act. Couldn't really deny this one.

I was taken to the police station. I didn't have to go far, they just walked me around the corner. Anyway, straight to the cells, sick as fuck. In the end I think there were around thirty arrested from Middlesbrough that day and they didn't have enough cells, so we were four to a cell. We had a right laugh about it. I was fined £100 for breach of the peace and carrying an offensive weapon (the brolly).

Some years later we made the trip to Huddersfield again with a similarly large mob, but we were intercepted by the police straight away and put in the nearest boozer which had three or four

Huddersfield lads in. I noticed one of them was a fat lad wearing glasses. I got talking to him and it only turned out he was the same lad who I had been arrested for, years before, and he was one of their top lads. Small world, eh?

As we drank in the boozer it was heaving with police outside, and we could see a large mob of Huddersfield boys. There was no chance of a kick-off though, as the police had it sussed. One of their lads, who was walking up and down in front of his mates with proper swagger about him, came across to the pub and the police let him in. He walked right through the middle of us with a right spring in his step. He must of thought he was King Dick. Anyway, he walked straight into the toilets and I followed close behind.

He was giving it, "Why don't you all come out and have it with us?"

I said, "If the police hadn't been swarming around we would have."

Then I thought, fuck you, cheeky cunt, and hit him with a cracking right hand. I launched him straight into the piss pots and then promptly left the toilets. He emerged a few minutes later, rubbing the side of his jaw. Everyone pissed themselves laughing at him. What made it worse was when he got back to his mates, we could see through the window he was explaining to them what had happened, and he was still rubbing his jaw. They all fell about laughing as well. He won't do that again in a hurry.

The rest of that day was pretty uneventful; the plod were taking no chances, swarmed us as soon as we left the boozer and never left our side until we were on the train going home.

ARSENAL

IN FEBRUARY, 1983, while we were waiting at the Cenotaph for the coach to pick us up to take us to Arsenal for a midweek FA cup replay, we were surprised to see Storky turn up. He had been released from Durham Prison a couple of hours earlier and his only worry was that we might have gone without him. If he had known what lay in store for him he would have stayed in his cell.

Arsenal had done nothing but hide behind the police escort the previous game and we were utterly disappointed with them and determined to take it to them. We arrived at the outskirts of London in the late afternoon and asked the driver to drop us off at King's Cross. He told us that he had to take us to an official coach park near Highbury, but when we stopped at traffic lights near Highgate tube station we got off, leaving him with an empty bus. There were only fifty of us so we headed up to King's Cross to pick up a few more lads who had travelled by train.

As we came up the escalators, on to the main platform, we noticed a few Arsenal spotters hanging around, trying to look cool. A few slaps were dished out to let them know we had arrived and they scurried off like rats. Looking back, we could have been a little more subtle, as we had also alerted the Met to our arrival. We headed towards the escalators and two of London's finest appeared and tried to force us on to the tube to Highbury. We had other plans and shot down on to another line with these muppets in pursuit.

We gathered on the platform and were picking our route to the Angel, where we knew we could have some fun, when to our surprise the two cops appeared on the platform and ordered us against the wall. There were a few blacks in our firm and the two coppers were screaming and shouting abuse at us, some of it racial. You could smell the tension as we looked up and down the platform in disbelief that these two mouthy coppers had tried to wrap us up on their own. Before I knew it, the two boys in blue were on the floor getting kicked to bits, they had pushed their luck and were paying for it.

When the kicking was over and the two were lying prone on the platform, a train pulled in, the doors opened and we all got on; all, that is, but one. The train idled for a few seconds with the doors open and, in his wisdom, Storky stayed on the platform to make sure everyone was on board. He liked to think of himself as a bit of a leader and stood over the two prone coppers giving out instructions. As the tube doors started to close, he went to jump on, but one of the coppers leapt up and rugby-tackled him to the floor. The doors shut and the train started to pull away as Storky tried to wriggle free while the rest of us fell about the train in hysterics. If it had been anyone else we would have stopped the train and helped him, but it was Storky and we pissed ourselves laughing. Those who knew him know why. Storky was one of Boro's top lads in the Eighties and was likeable enough, but if you turned your back he would have your eyeballs out. He would pinch anything off anybody. On this occasion he was arrested and was beaten black and blue by the police.

Years later, in the mid-Nineties, Storky was living in York and during a burglary he allegedly killed a pensioner. He went on the run with the police one step behind him and was eventually found dead in a flat. He had taken a heroin overdose. Nobody knew whether it was an accident or he had done it intentionally. I think the latter, because if he had been caught for the pensioner's death he'd have been looking at a life sentence, but nobody really knows.

We had to get off this train fast or be nicked, so at the next stop we were off and came out on Highbury Corner. A few police on horseback tried to contain us but we easily slipped by them and were now on the streets with no OB in tow. We made our way to the ground without much trouble and, as we got closer, we started to run into a few little mobs that were swiftly dealt with. We arrived at the ground and could not believe how easy it was to walk around with no opposition. To try this at Ayresome Park would be suicide.

As we walked past the entrance to the North Bank we spotted a few of the lads we had seen earlier at King's Cross. Again, a few slaps and they were off, running away from their own end. There was nothing doing so we went in the ground and into the seats next to the fence that separated us from the North Bank. We soon attracted their mob and they came to the fence to shout abuse and the usual bollocks, while we sat and laughed at them.

Half-time arrived and together we went down under the stand on the off chance of a confrontation. We were not to be disappointed. At first it was the usual, people getting drinks and stuff and we stood around letting everyone know who we were. The crowd was starting to head back to the seats and the numbers were starting to thin, but in the distance we could see a few likely looking lads staring at us. As we moved closer to them, their numbers started to rise and they came towards us, then, bang, it was off, both mobs tore into each other. The fighting only lasted a few seconds but it was a furious encounter with honours even.

THE BRICK

Before we knew it, the OB were swarming all over us. We were wrapped up and put in the Boro end and had to pass through the lads who we'd just had it with. They told us where to go after the match if we wanted more, and, of course, we did.

We were held back for twenty minutes until the crowd outside had cleared and when we were let out the streets were almost deserted. We had no idea where our bus was parked and no-one seemed to care as we slipped by the police and headed off down an empty street. After about ten minutes we came to a tube station. One stop away was Holloway Road, where Arsenals' mob had told us to go, so we headed off there, as we knew there were also few pubs in that area. As we got off the tube and made our way up the stairs, a few Arsenal lads coming in the opposite direction spotted us and turned and ran back up to the top of the stairs. We went after them but when we got close to the top we were showered with bottles and whatever else they could get their hands on. Finally, we made it to the top of the stairs and out on to the street. The Arsenal had bolted, so we checked out the pubs but had no luck their either.

Their main mob never arrived, but we did have small skirmishes right through till about 10pm with small pockets of lads. Finally the police arrived, well pissed off with us as we had been giving them the runaround all night. We were put up against a wall while they tried to locate our coach, a few liberties were taken and a few slaps were dished out, no surprise I suppose. We were held for about an hour before our bus finally turned up, the driver looked well pissed-off with us as we took our seats for a long journey home.

BOLTON

THIS STORY WAS written by one of Middlesbrough's top lads. He wishes to remain anonymous.

My first trip to Bolton was a complete nightmare, a league game in 1983. We hired a van, got there early, parked near the station and went looking for a pub. We had only been out of the van for about a minute when a small group of lads on the other side of the road started staring. A few words were exchanged so we crossed over to them and kicked it off. A few punches and it was over as they backed off, but out of the blue a copper appeared waving his truncheon, and then, wallop, the cunt smashed it over my shoulder, knocking me to the ground. He then pinned me down and cuffed me. The rest of the lads gathered round us and the copper shit himself because he thought he was in for a kicking, but he had no need to worry as a police van sped up the road to his rescue. It must have only been about 12.30.

They bundled me into the van and took me to the ground. For a second I thought they were going to let me go. How wrong! Outside the ground was a big police wagon with a dozen or so little cells in the back. I was put in one and left there until after the game.

Five hours later, when they finally took me to the police station, I was numb from the waist down and I couldn't feel the fingers on my left hand after the knock on the shoulder. After another hour in the station cells they charged me and kicked me out. They had to as I had the van keys and the rest of the lads were hanging around outside waiting for me.

I was already on a suspended sentence and was sent to Strangeways for four months. There were a few Bolton lads in the court and we got talking. A couple of them also got sent down and during my stay in that piss-stinking shithole I became good friends with them. A couple of years later I was back inside and found myself deposited in HMP Haverigg, where I bumped into one of the Bolton lads and again we became good friends.

Strangeways had all the dregs of society. You were banged up in your cell for twenty-three hours a day, with an hour's exercise once a day. You had to piss or shit in a bucket and then slop out on the morning in the toilet, or recess area, as it was called. The smell of a morning in the recess area was sickening. You had to then fill the bowl they gave you with water to take back to your cell to wash in. The rules were Victorian and had stuck and never changed.

The Boro had been relegated to the Third Division by now and, by all accounts, the lads were having a great time on their travels, I couldn't wait to get out and join them. Bolton were also in the Third Division and were due to play us in a few months when me and my Bolton mate would both be free. We made our plans and kept in touch after our release until the time came. On the night before the game I travelled to Bolton and spent the night with my old mate. We went into town and drank with their lads all night. I kept quiet at first but as the night grew longer I opened up and made myself known to their mob. Most of them were sound and told me where they would be and how to get there and so on.

In the morning I made the short journey to Victoria Station in Manchester and was surprised to find 100 of our lads already there. I told them the plan of attack and in no time I was back in Bolton town centre. There were no police at the station as we made our way out and off towards the meet, which was an underground snooker hall. As we approached we saw a few Bolton lads hanging around and one shouted over to us that we were too early and they had no lads out yet. It was about twelve o'clock so we shot into the nearest pub for a beer. After half an hour, one of the lads that I had been drinking with the night before came in the pub and explained that if we left for another pub, the Sweet Green Tavern, about half a mile away they would meet us for an off. We agreed and left in dribs and drabs but there was no sign of their mob and a few of our lads were beginning to think this was all a waste of time.

We managed to get to the pub undetected and waited. After an hour there was still no sign of them. The pub was facing the opposite way to the town centre so we could not see them coming, so every five minutes I went out and had a look around the back. It was starting to look like a no show and the lads were questioning the logic of staying put. Once again I went outside to see if there was any sign of them – and almost walked straight into them.

There must have been more than 200 spread out across the road, trying to come behind the pub from both sides. A few were only ten yards from me and I should have retreated back to the front of the pub to alert the lads, but I couldn't resist a pop. I ran forward and got two good shots in on one lad, which wobbled him, and then turned to leg it to the front of the pub with a huge snarling mob on my tail. As I turned towards the entrance I ran into a load of Bolton who had come around the other side. I was fucked. A couple of our lot were drinking in the pub doorway and I screamed at them to get the lads out. They didn't need telling twice. I was now in the middle of the road with Bolton bearing down on me from both sides and the lad who I had just punched making straight for me. Before I knew it they were swarming all over me and I was soon on the floor getting punched and kicked.

Then there was a loud roar followed by a loud crash. The lads poured out of the pub and Bolton backed off in two big groups to allow them out. This gave me time to get to my feet and I stood for a second trying to assess the situation. The pub window had been put through from the inside by the Boro who could not get out quick enough. Glasses and stools were being thrown through the window into the street and more and more lads were pouring through the door. There were enough of us out to take them on and we went straight at them. The fight was on two fronts and it was furious. This wasn't one of those fights where just the lads at the front got stuck in with those at the back making a load of noise; everyone was in.

I lost my position and seemed to be surrounded by Bolton and the noise was deafening as both mobs went at it. The first few police arrived but not enough of them and we kept on going with the police running amongst us, lashing out like they were enjoying it. We started to get on top as one of the Bolton mobs backed off and we turned and concentrated our efforts on the remaining mob. Soon we had them off and the battle was over as more police arrived. They were well pissed off with us and loads of Boro got knocked about. We were rounded up in a no-nonsense style and escorted to the ground where we went on to win the game 1–0 to complete another top day out.

A few days later I received a letter from my Bolton mate congratulating us for a good show. He also sent me the press cuttings from their local rag with a picture of the pub in a right old state, but best of all was a statement from the pub landlord who claimed the Boro fans were perfectly behaved and never a problem, bless him.

MOTORWAY MADNESS

MIDWAY THROUGH THE Eighties we had an away fixture with Chelsea. Over the years we had developed a lot of history with them and had become arch-rivals, so I knew everybody would be up for this one. Mind you, we had developed a lot of history with all the top clubs in the country. This is what happens when you are one of the top mobs.

Although we are not a major city, not even close, we have been mentioned in nearly every football hooligan book that has been published. We are just a small town in the North East of England, but what a violent town. Twenty years of going to games and many, many years on the door has taught me this. People always say to me, if you want trouble in Middlesbrough you will get it. Only sometimes you get it when you don't. Somebody once told me that in the First World War there were more Teessiders killed on the front line than any other soldiers from any other part of the country. It just goes to show we were game as fuck all those years ago.

Anyway, back to Chelsea. Everybody had been going on about this game for ages. We all congregated at the Cenotaph, waiting to be picked up by the coach. There was a proper buzz about the place because everybody knew what lay in store when we got to

THE BRICK

London. We left Middlesbrough around 6.30am and the bus was full of our top lads. Everybody was in high spirits, as we always were on Saturdays. We joined the A1 South and soon pulled into the first service station we came across. Everyone walked straight into the shopping area and it was like Ali Baba and the Forty Thieves, hilarious to watch. Everybody crammed their jackets with just about anything and everything that wasn't nailed down, sandwiches, sweets, teddy bears, fanny mags, you name it, it was stolen. We boarded the coach and, on the A1, everybody was throwing sweets at each other and getting brayed over the head with teddy bears. It's childish, I know, but it was funny at the time.

A couple of hours later we pulled into Leicester Forest service station. A couple of our lads went over the bridge to the shops on the opposite side of the motorway. While we were on our side doing a bit of "shopping", the two lads ran back over the bridge and shouted, "There's a coach load of QPR travelling to Grimsby on the other side, and it's all their top lads." Everybody stopped what they were doing and ran over the bridge to have it with them. We came down into the foyer area and were met by fifty of QPR's firm.

They didn't know what the fuck was happening. We ran straight at them. Bins were flying, canned drinks, anything we could get our hands on. There were lads all over the foyer area and the punches and kicks were dished out like they were going out of fashion. They backed off and were on their toes back through the doors into the car park area. We followed and it started going off again. I remember chucking a can of Coke at one lad and bingo, hit him clean in the dial. I bet that put him off Coke for a while.

I looked to my right and one of my mates was on the floor with four QPR all over him. As I ran over to help him the lads backed off because all the Boro had come running forward again. What I saw at this point really shocked me. They had slashed him with a blade from the corner of his mouth to right behind his ear. His face was wide open and you could see his gums and teeth through the hole. The funny thing is, all he could say was, "Leave me alone and go and get into them."

By this time the police had arrived and were swarming all over. The QPR fans all got back on their bus but I just saw red. I pulled a Stanley knife out of my pocket and ran at the QPR coach. What I was going to do I wasn't sure, but it seemed the right thing to do at the time. Just as I was boarding the coach, knife in hand, I was dragged back by two coppers who arrested me straight away.

I heard later that they had searched the QPR bus and found nothing and let them go on their way. Imagine that happening today: everyone would have been locked up, forensics would have been involved, and there would have been some serious jail dished out. Like I said earlier, you could get away with murder at football in those days.

I never got to Chelsea that day. I was let out of Leicester Police Station around 6pm and charged with carrying an offensive weapon. Eventually, I was fined £75 for carrying the blade and the magistrates told me I was a thug and a hooligan. I thought to myself, yeah, yeah, yeah, wait until we meet QPR again and I'll show you who's a thug.

The lad who was slashed spent some time in hospital and had a massive amount of stitches and clips to the inside and outside of his face.

THE BRICK

The following was written by another of Middlesbrough's top lads. He wishes to remain anonymous.

We were at Portsmouth on the opening day of the 1984–85 season. At the same fixture the year before we had gone down in dribs and drabs and been surprised at the number of lads they had. There were hundreds and they were well up for it. At the time we were not a big mob, we had several groups who all wanted to do their own thing.

Our group decided to drive down in a minibus and six or seven cars. We met up outside Rumours nightclub after closing time and headed off down the A1 at about 3 a.m. This was not to everyone's liking and was why we only numbered around fifty. The first stop was a service station on the M1. As we pulled in some of the lads got into an argument with a few miners on their way to a picket line. These were big, angry-looking fuckers who were spoiling for a fight, and we obliged. The first few punches went in and, give these blokes their due, they were game as fuck. More lads from both sides joined in and the fight spread around the car park. It stopped when the rest of our mob pulled in and we had the numbers on them and they backed off. We could have gone after them but we knew plod would be along soon and decided to get back on the motorway as our fight was not with this lot.

With spirits high we headed off down the M1 to Leicester Forest service station and parked up a bit before seven o'clock. Most of the lads were sleeping off the beer in the cars but as I had not had a drink I walked up to the cafeteria for a coffee, where another half dozen were doing the same. A few more went across to the other side of the services and bumped into a group of Southampton lads on their way to Sunderland. Two of our lads knew a few of this mob from working down there a few months previously. A few words were said and our lads returned to the café and told me that this lot were up for an early morning row if we were. We decided to oblige and walked over to take a look.

38

Thirty of them were spread out in a line just outside the entrance to the services at the bottom of the stairs. There were about ten of us and, quietly, I told one of our lads to inform the rest that the football season was about to start early, then I turned to our lads and said, "Lets go." I walked up to one of the Southampton, who had his arms folded, trying to make his biceps look big, and punched him flush on the jaw. That was it, it was off. As I continued punching I could hear the familiar shouts and screams behind me as the rest of the lads got stuck into each other.

We were fighting for a good thirty seconds or so when I heard someone yell, "Blades, watch the fucking blades." At that, I pulled away from the lad I was fighting and stepped back. The whole fight seemed to stop at once. In front of me was a lad with his arms down by his side, just standing there, staring at me. I looked down and could see a blade in his right hand. To be honest, he looked like he didn't know how to use it, but what I didn't know was that he already had, on me!

The sight of a blade does things to you and we backed off through the doors and into the building, where we armed ourselves with whatever we could get our hands on, bins, signs, anything; this fight was not over yet. Southampton started coming through the doors, I steamed back into them, the roar went up and it went off again. We were inside the building now and the noise was echoing off the walls, it was total chaos with objects flying around, bodies bouncing about, shouting and fighting. I had been fighting for what seemed like ten minutes, even though it was more like two, and was absolutely fucked and could hardly breathe. I let go of the lad I was battling with and stepped back against a wall. My opponent was also knackered and backed off towards the doors. As I stood there, fighting for breath, I looked up at the stairs and was glad to see some more of our lads arrive. The Brick and a few others came bouncing down the stairs straight into them.

Southampton backed off into the car park with our lads after them. The first police sirens could now be heard and a police car screeched up right outside the doors. It was time to leave. I was still against the wall when one of the lads pointed at my chest. I looked down to see a small circle of blood on my tee-shirt. I lifted it up and found an inch-long stab wound directly over my heart. I was in no pain and quickly got myself back to the cars on the other side of the motorway. As I sat in the minibus I was fortunate to be surrounded by medical experts who reliably informed me that it was fuck all. The blade had hit a rib and, although I needed to get it cleaned up, I was OK.

We had to leave and agreed to meet up at Watford Gap service station. At this point one of the lads asleep in the bus woke up and asked where he was. He had only got on the bus for a lift home from the nightclub. We all pissed ourselves laughing and welcomed him along to Portsmouth. We pulled into the services and I went to get first aid. As I was getting patched up I noticed a Transit van in the car park getting some attention from a few of ours. A fight broke out so, in the middle of getting bandaged up, I ran out into the car park. The van had about a dozen Man City lads on board and the driver decided to do one and sped off with the rear doors open. One of our more notorious lads jumped on the back of the van and aimed kicks at it as he clung to the roof. Once again we had to leave prematurely and headed off for the next service station. Unfortunately, as we pulled in our convoy was clocked by a traffic patrol car, which meant they were onto us, so we got off the motorway and drove into London.

Somehow, we managed to stay together as we drove down the Edgware Road then, out of the blue, a patrol car swooped on us. They managed to stop a few of the cars and when more police turned up we knew it was over for the day. I was not stopped and drove off in search of a hospital, found one in Hammersmith and nipped in for a few stitches. But by the time they sorted me out it was 4pm and I never did get to Portsmouth.

THE BARNSLEY
MASSACRE

IN FEBRUARY, 1984, we played Barnsley at Ayresome Park. I
was a young lad and up-and-coming hooligan so I would attend
all home matches, even if it was somebody like Barnsley, where
we thought there would be no trouble. I always went on the off-
chance there would be trouble. Barnsley have never ever been
associated with football violence, however, this particular
Saturday they would be associated with it whether they liked it
or not.

I wanted to be in town early so I could meet the lads and see
what Barnsley had to offer. Some of you will know the feeling you
get on a Saturday morning when you know you have a game to go
to, especially when you know the team you are playing have a
violent reputation. It's a real buzz, that funny adrenalin feeling in
your stomach, a nice feeling really. You have to pay £40 a gram for
that same feeling these days. Somehow, I didn't get the feeling on
this morning, because Barnsley were not really associated with
violence, but this was all about to change.

I arrived in town and met up with a few of the lads who told
me that Barnsley had a large mob in the Wellington Pub on

THE BRICK

Albert Road. Albert Road is right in the town centre, runs from the train station up to the main shopping precinct and is lined with pubs. The Wellington is at the end of the road. I was quite shocked that Barnsley had brought a proper mob and had arrived so early, because not many teams have done this at Middlesbrough, even up to this day. So we knew we had to make sure they received a proper Middlesbrough welcome.

A handful of us walked past the Wellington and we were going to go inside so see what the crack was but they had doormen and the doors were locked. One of us jumped on to a GPO green box outside the window and confirmed there were around sixty lads inside from their main mob. We were very surprised. We returned to the other lads and told them what we had seen. There were thirty or forty of us at the most. We didn't have the numbers to match Barnsley but the mob that we did have would have stood their own against anyone.

We went into a pub just a little further up from the Wellington, on the other side of the road, providing a perfect view if they decided to come out and make a show. We had a couple of drinks and waited for the rest of our lads to come into town, but with us playing Barnsley, I think most of our lads weren't interested. Some of our lads went up to the Wellington and taunted the Barnsley mob through the window. If this had been today, the pub would have been swarming with police, but with it being the early Eighties there wasn't a copper in sight. It was brilliant for us, but would become a nightmare for them.

While we were waiting for them to make a show, three of our lads had a walk round to Woollies and stole some Stanley knives. No-one was surprised by what they had brought back, because in the early Eighties every mob carried Stanley knives at football. It was like a fashion accessory and part of being a football hooligan. Everyone seemed to carry them, and we were no different.

As we stood outside the pub at around 1.30pm we heard banging coming from the Wellington and suddenly the doors burst open. The Barnsley mob spilled out onto the pavement and spread out into Albert Road. If only they knew what lay in store for them they would have stayed where they where. In fact, if they knew what lay in store for them they would probably have stayed at home. They were shouting, "Come on Boro," an invitation we couldn't refuse. We came out of the pub opposite still without a copper in sight – a hooligan's dream.

Although we were outnumbered, this was our town and there was no way they were getting away with this. Running was totally out of the question. We never did anyway, that's why we were one of the best mobs around. We met head-on in the middle of Albert Road, fists and feet were flying and there was a lot of shouting. At first Barnsley seemed really game and the fighting went on for some time. Each mob was giving as good as they were getting – it was a proper off. A few more of our lads came up from behind them, so we were now on both sides of their mob and they were trapped in the middle, the filling in a Barnsley sandwich if you like.

I was in the thick of it, dishing out rights and lefts as quick as I possibly could. All the lads were going at it hammer and tongs and then, all of a sudden, there seemed to be a panic amongst the Barnsley mob. I could hear people shouting, "He's been stabbed, he's been stabbed," and the Barnsley mob started to back off. They were trying to beat a hasty retreat back into the Wellington but one of its doors was shut and the number of people trying to get through a narrow door created a bottleneck. The Barnsley mob were now in blind panic and I was about to find out why. While we were still attacking them I can remember one lad stood in front of me in total panic. He had been slashed across his forehead and he had a gaping wound from one side to the other.

The blood was pissing out and he was covered from head to foot. It looked like something out of a horror movie.

As I turned I saw another lad running about like a chicken with no head. He had also been slashed right down his arm from top to bottom and he was screaming for help. I thought, it's not help you need mate, it's a fucking arm transplant. The blood was dripping off the ends of his fingers and his jumper was wide open from the shoulder to the wrist. The pavement was quickly turning red and it looked like a murder scene. As I turned the make a sharp exit I saw a third lad who had also been slashed across the back of his neck and was screaming for help.

Although I had been in some proper offs at football, I knew this was different and I knew I had to get away as quickly as possible. This was serious shit, not your run-of-the-mill football violence. This was on a completely different level. As I made my way up Albert Road I was having to hop over pools of blood. I ran as fast as my legs would carry me, with all the other Boro lads thinking the same. As we got to the top of Albert Road we turned right into the main shopping precinct and could hear police sirens coming from everywhere. We were panicking that we were going to get nicked, police cars were flying all over the town centre and it was obvious that they had realised the full extent of what we had done and were trying to round up the people responsible. We split up into twos and threes and just blended in with Saturday shoppers. We thought going up to Ayresome Park would be a bad idea so stayed in the centre for a while, but in the end we decided to go anyway. All the way up to the ground coppers were driving up and down the side streets, obviously looking to nick people.

We were not far from the ground when a van pulled up and about half a dozen coppers jumped out.

"Can I just have a word with you lads?"

"No problem," I said. "What's wrong?"

I was trying to act as innocent as I could but under the circumstances I must have looked as guilty as fuck.

"Have you two been into town today?" the copper asked.

Trying to stay calm I said, "No mate, we've just got off the bus in Linthorpe Road." I was shitting myself but was trying to bluff it out.

"Okay lads, on your way," he said.

We walked off and I was thinking to myself, thick cunt, you'll never make a Sherlock Holmes. As we walked up the side streets we thought we had got away with it, but little did I know what lay ahead.

We went into the seats behind the goal in the East Stand. There were coppers everywhere, both uniformed and in plain clothes. They were all on their radios at the same time. It's a wonder the airways weren't jammed. Right the way throughout the game they were nicking people, so when the final whistle came I was very relieved. We left the ground and, safely outside, we thought we had got away with it. At that particular time we thought the whole thing was funny.

We knew we were going to hit the headlines for this one but we didn't realise how big it would be. All we were bothered about at the time was sending a message out to other mobs up and down the country, "You can't come to Middlesbrough mob-handed and get away with it."

When I arrived home I turned on the television and, fuck me, we had hit the headlines all right. I was shocked at what I was hearing. Details were a bit sketchy because it had only happened a few hours before, but what they knew was that four people had been badly slashed, one right across his forehead, one the full length of his arm, one across the back of his neck and one across his forearm. Three of these lads needed immediate blood transfusions and were now seriously ill in hospital. This was serious and I knew it. I thought to myself it would only be a matter of time before the inevitable knock on the door would come.

I quickly got changed and made my way back into town where everyone was talking about what had happened. Nothing like this had ever happened at Middlesbrough before, so it was big news. By all accounts four of the lads who had been involved with us had already been nicked. We talked about who would be next to get nicked and took the piss out of each other, saying that the other person would be next. We still thought it was funny, but not for long.

The next day all the Sunday papers were full of headlines like "Blood Bath" and "Attempted Murder". This was now major league stuff and I knew I was in deep shit. I wished it would all go away but what was done was done and I was going to pay the price.

Monday morning came and, you guessed it, bang, bang, bang on the door. Isn't it funny that ten people could knock on your door at different times and knock differently every time but you automatically know when it's the police. They must teach them how to do a Policeman's Knock at the Academy. Criminals and hooligans must have a built-in sensor which tells you it's the police at the door. Bang, bang, bang, went the door again and I did what any normal person would do, I pulled the quilt right back over my head and thought, fuck you, officer. After a while they must have got sick of it because they left but I knew it would only be a matter of time before they returned. After all, four lads nearly died. This was no daft breach of the peace charge, this was heavy stuff and, boy, did I know it.

Twice more they came back and the first time I didn't answer. The second time I climbed out of the landing window on to the garage roof and my brother, Mark, let them into the house. They searched it from top to bottom, even the loft. When it became obvious I wasn't there, they left. If only they had looked out of the window, I was laid on the garage roof, four feet away. That all changed one morning when they came early and my dad had gone to work and forgot to lock the back door. I was woken up by two CID officers, not a nice sight first thing in the morning. I have woken up next to some pigs on a morning but this was different. I was arrested and cautioned. They threw all kinds of offences at me like stabbing, slashing and malicious wounding. This was nine days after the offences had taken place and I knew loads of the lads had been interviewed so I knew my name had been mentioned.

At the nick I denied being there, I even denied being in the town that day but I was pissing against the wind because several statements were read out to me, placing me outside the pub when it went off. I was one of the last ones to get nicked so the cops knew I had been there and taken part. I was interviewed a number of times and eventually charged with affray. Finally, thirteen of us were charged with offences ranging from malicious wounding, affray and assault to carrying offensive weapons. They threw the fucking book at us.

At the time we were all young lads and being as we were, we thought it was one big joke. I know now, looking back, how serious it was. I mean, four people nearly lost their lives, but at that time we didn't give a flying fuck. We appeared in court several times and it was adjourned again and again. We knew this was going to be a big case as there were hundreds of witnesses and a lot of paperwork to sort out. The Crown Court date was set for trial in mid-November, 1984. We were all placed on curfews and had to sign on at the police station every Saturday afternoon. When we eventually got to court we all stood in the dock and, to be honest, still thought it was one big joke. All but two of us pleaded not guilty. I was taught from an early age never to admit to anything, even if you get accused of pinching sweets and you had chocolate all round your mouth. They had to prove it, I was told, and so I stuck to this rigidly. In the end it didn't do me any good but God loves a trier.

Every day we turned up at Crown Court and were bailed every night to go home. None of us knew how serious this case was turning out to be. All we did, right through the trial, was take the piss out of the witnesses and laugh. I can't remember how many times the judge told us to stop messing about. It was just ammunition for him if we were found guilty to absolutely nail us. He was Judge Angus Stroyen, a judge not to be messed with, by all accounts, and in front of him were thirteen young football hooligans charged with half killing four people and all we could do was piss about. He must have been fucking boiling. Never mind, he got his revenge when all of us were found guilty.

Talk about getting your arse reamed, the thirteen of us received a total of thirty-nine years in jail. Do not pick up £200 and do not pass Go. Straight to jail we went. I was wounded. Not as wounded as the Barnsley four but wounded nonetheless. Sentences ranged from six years down to five, four, three, two and eighteen months. I received two years with an extra year to run concurrent for a couple of daft theft charges they had thrown in for good measure. The way the jail system worked in those days I would be spending the next sixteen months in youth custody unless I got parole and then I would be out in eight. We awaited sentencing in the bridewell, that's the cells underneath the court. They called the first four up and fifteen minutes later, when they walked back through the door, they looked like they had seen a ghost. Between the four of them they had received twenty years. When they told us this, we fell about laughing, but that stopped when it was our turn. Judge Stroyen said it was the worst case of football violence he had ever witnessed and we were called hooligans and thugs.

During the sixteen-day trial, two hundred witnesses were called, ranging from the full Barnsley mob to the pub landlord, doormen, Saturday shoppers and shopkeepers. Every witness was asked if they were frightened. When each said, "Yes," I knew we were fucked.

It's funny how things turn out, because a number of years later I worked as a doorman on the same pub where it happened. To this day, this is the worst punishment in terms of years given out by a single judge for football violence. I was nineteen years old, my girlfriend at the time was three months pregnant, I had never been to jail before and here I was staring two years inside right in the face. The thing that didn't make it seem so bad at the time was that some of the lads received larger sentences than me, so I thought I had got quite a good deal in the end, if you can call two years in jail a good deal. We all left the cells that night and went straight to Durham Jail or the "Big House", as it was called. I wondered what lay ahead.

HER MAJESTY'S HOTEL

DURHAM JAIL LOOKED like Colditz. None of us had been to prison before, so we were about to find out first hand what lay in store for us. The first thing we noticed was the size of the cameras on the walls. There'd be no escape attempts from here – not by us, anyway. We were ushered into the reception area and told to take a bath. Your own clothes are taken from you and you are issued with prison clothes, not the smartest of attire, especially when you are used to wearing designer gear. "You lot must be the football hooligans then," said one of the screws. It had been in the papers every day for sixteen days right through the trial, so they were expecting us. We were issued with plastic knives and forks and a plastic cup, and it was off to our cells.

When you walk on to the landing in Durham, the thing that hits you is the smell. There's a pungent, strange odour that I can only describe as a mixture of piss and vomit. Not the nicest smell, I can assure you. I was put in a single cell and the door was slammed shut behind me. Fucking nice, this, I thought. The cell stank. I think it was then that it hit me. I was wounded.

The next morning we were let out for breakfast, but how can they call it breakfast? Surely they can be done under the Trade

51

Descriptions Act. Fucking breakfast, I thought wryly to myself, can't wait for dinner. The food was shite and because I was in a single cell there was no one to talk to. We were let out once a day for about an hour to walk around the exercise yard. There was a footpath in a big square, and you had to just walk round and round like some caged animal. Mind you, I suppose that's what we were really. On a Sunday everyone could go to church and as it meant an extra hour out of your cell, everybody went. It's the only time I have every gone to church and looked forward to it, me being dead religious and all that.

The weeks passed and eventually, after five weeks being banged up every day for twenty-three hours, we were to be transferred to a Youth Custody Centre. Half were going to Castington in Northumberland, and the other half, including me, were going to Deerbolt Youth Custody in Barnard Castle. It was totally different to Durham. We were placed on open units where there were four landings with fifteen lads on each landing. You had your own key to your own door and they used to lock the landing at the end so you could come and go as you pleased on the landing; a big difference from twenty-three hours locked up. I was a young lad and, to be honest, they could have thrown anything at me and I would not have been bothered. Deerbolt wasn't a hard detention centre; the regime was pretty relaxed, so we took full advantage of it. I think at one time about half of Deerbolt's population was made up of lads from Middlesbrough, and most of them were football hooligans.

On the first morning, I went down and walked along the serving hatch. The lad who was serving the porridge was on the same landing as me and when I held my tray out he put the smallest scoop of porridge on it. I looked at him and said, "Howay mate, a full scoop." He just ignored me, as if to say, "Fuck you." I'd made my first enemy. I thought to myself, wait until we get back on the landing you little shit. He must have taken a dislike to me for some strange reason.

Once we were back on the landing the screw locked us in and was gone. I walked straight to the lad's cell and said, "I need to talk to you mate." He opened his door. "Big mistake," I said to him. "Whack" – I right-handed him and he staggered back into his cell. I quickly followed and for good measure stamped on his head a few times. I'd just sent a message to everyone on my landing that I wouldn't take shit off anyone. I expected him to grass me up and thought I would lose some days through a Governor's report, but give him his due, he never did. He had a beauty of a black eye though.

I quickly established myself on the landing as "one of the lads" and settled in pretty quickly. I had to really, after all I was doing two years. Some of the bullying that went on in Deerbolt was unbelievable. If you showed a weakness in any way you were tortured. Youth Custody Centre or YC is no place for the weak; it was survival of the fittest. Being young, I just went along with it. When new lads came onto the landing, if they turned out to be idiots – and believe me there was a lot of them – then they were tortured. Soap, shampoo, toothpaste, would be taken off them and these three things are precious to you inside.

Everyone was issued with a Yale key to their cell but you had to remember to double lock it when you were out. If you didn't and you just pulled the door shut, it could be opened by sliding a piece of plastic up near the lock, similar to a credit card, and remember, the place was full of thieves. Loads of times I saw idiots not locking their doors behind them when they went to association or the canteen shop. They learned the hard way. As soon as their backs were turned then their doors were opened and the cells ransacked. Lads would be fighting with each other over who was going to be first in to get the best stuff.

THE BRICK

We had a cell inspection every Sunday morning and anybody who was weak, or a total shitbag, used to clean and polish all the lads' cells. We'd have been fucked if they got caught in our cells, especially cleaning them, because bullying wasn't tolerated, but it was rife all over the Centre. When new inmates arrived, if they were one of the lads nowt happened, but if they were weak then it was hell for them. People used to get what we called blanket jobs. About four or five would wait outside someone's cell with a blanket and somebody would knock on the door. As soon as the door was opened the blanket would be wrapped round the lad's head and he would be kicked to fuck. Sometimes it was for no reason at all, except for a bit of entertainment.

Any signs of weakness were sussed out straight away and it was always the same few every week were cleaning everyone's cells for inspection. When these idiots were due for release, the night before they left would be absolute hell. They were systematically humiliated in front of the other lads, just for entertainment. Their trousers and underpants were stripped off and their balls and arses boot-polished with black wax polishes. It made a right mess and it was a nightmare trying to get the polish off because all we had on the landing were four sinks, the showers were downstairs and the landings were locked for the night.

The lads getting out also used to get stripped naked and put inside a kitbag with the top tied. They'd be left on the landing for ages. When they were in the kitbags and couldn't see anything, if one of the lads had a grudge or had taken a dislike to the lad in the bag, or if someone just felt like it, punches or kicks would be dished out without warning.

We had a riot button on the end of the landing which alerted the main office and would bring all the screws running on to the landing. Most of the time they would find a kitbag with someone inside it struggling to get out, while we would all have disappeared back into our rooms. The best time for the riot bell was winter, as the main office was across a large tarmac yard. When it had snowed or it was very icy, someone would press the button and we would all watch from the windows as the screws ran across the yard and sometimes went on their arses. We would crack up laughing and by the time they got to the landing, everyone was in their rooms pretending to be doing something or other. They would tell everyone to come on to the landing and stand by their doors and ask, "Who pressed the riot bell?" Obviously, no-one ever owned up, so they made us miss association for a couple of nights as punishment. I lost count how many times this happened but it never ever stopped the carry on.

Another funny thing that used to happen all the time was every couple of hours during the night a nightwatchman unlocked the landing, walked to the other end, placed a key in a box and turned it to show he had checked the landing. When he was down the end of the landing someone would shout, "Night-watchman." He would shout back, "Who is it?" and someone would shout, "Your lass is getting fucked while you're at work, you silly old cunt." He would go off it because he didn't know who it was and, when he went to where he thought the voice was coming from, someone else would shout from the other end of the landing. It wound him up no end.

One lad, who was a bit depressed for some reason or other, wanted to go home. We told him if he cut his wrist with a razor he would go to hospital and they might let him go home. Yeah, like fuck, but he believed us anyway. I remember him sitting there trying to cut himself and he wasn't doing it deep enough. Someone said, "Just hack it, but you've got to do it hard." I know it wasn't very nice but I've never got any awards for being nice previously, so I wasn't arsed. Next thing he'd only cut through the artery. Fucking hell, have you ever seen anybody with an artery cut? Not a nice sight. He panicked, blood was spurting out all over. Somebody pressed the riot bell on the wall at the end of the landing and everyone did a runner back to their cells. The screws were in there for about ten minutes wrapping his arm up and then he was taken to the Medical Centre. Did he go home? Did he fuck! He lost twenty-eight days remission and was back on the landing in the same cell within a week. He quickly learned not to listen to us again, but like I said, "That's entertainment."

Another time a skinny, blond-haired lad who, to be honest, looked like a faggot, came on to our landing. He was from Cramlington, near Newcastle, and another lad who lived near him and knew him told us that he was a bit of a nance and had been caught with his cock in a Hoover. I know, I laughed as well when I first heard it. Anyway, as you can guess, we christened him "Hoover Fucker" and, by Christ, he took some stick, poor cunt. Now Hoover Fucker, not being the brightest light on the tree, just went along with it all. I bet he never committed another offence, but I can't say whether or not he sexually assaulted a Dyson ever again. Anyway, he was tortured from day one. He used to polish everyone's cell floor and make everybody's bed packs for inspection.

One time it got really bad. We were all in bed one night at about 11pm and everyone was in their individual cells on the open landing. Somebody shouted from inside their cell, "Hoover Fucker, come here." No response.

"Hoover Fucker, come here."

"What do you want?" came the reply.

"Come to my door, I want you."

I heard a cell door open, obviously Hoover Fucker, and the sound of his footsteps as he walked to the door of the lad who had been shouting him. Then there was the sound of another cell door opening and, "Smack".

"Now get back to bed Hoover Fucker, you daft cunt."

This carried on for about half an hour as different lads on the landing shouted him, and every time he got up and went to their door and got whacked. You had to be there. Like I said, I've never got any awards for being nice.

One time I remember a lad in the recess called Hoover Fucker to the toilet area. The lad was having a shit and told Hoover Fucker to wipe his arse. Hoover Fucker walked away and I thought no more of it. About thirty seconds later he came back with a toilet roll and knocked on the toilet door. As you can imagine we cracked up laughing. He never did wipe the lad's arse, but we knew we could ask him to do anything, and he would. We fully exploited this and had him doing all sorts, mainly for entertainment.

We told him one night he could smash his cell window, climb out with a knotted blanket and then run for the fence. He fell for this hook, line and sinker. I don't know if he thought he would get away, I suspect he'd just had enough of us. He knew if he got caught he'd go to a secure unit where each cell door was locked individually, and so he'd get peace. We told everyone on the unit he was going to do it and, sure enough, after association, 8.30 came and he smashed the window. He climbed out and headed straight for the fence, blanket in tow. He didn't even get to the fence before he was roughly tackled. He lost twenty-eight days and went straight to the secure. I wish we hadn't told him to do it, it spoilt our fun. Never mind, there's hundreds of his type in jail, so we soon had someone else doing our cells out for inspection and polishing our shoes.

A couple of the lads who'd been sentenced with me had received eighteen months and were due for parole. They had served nearly six months would be out in a matter of weeks if they got parole. They went before the Governor and each was told they had been successful and were to be released. Nice one, I thought. That meant that if they had their parole then I would most certainly get mine. After all, I was in for the same offence.

A couple more weeks passed and one of the lads, who had just three days to go before he was due to leave, was caught by the screws bullying another inmate. He and others had dragged the victim into the toilet area and pushed a broom shank up his sleeve and then across his back and out the other sleeve, so he was in a crucifix position. They then tied him to the skylight grill so he was just hanging off the floor. Once he was in this position they took his trousers and undies off and boot-polished his bollocks and arse. Things started to get out of hand and he was punched and kicked, and eventually had his teeth brushed with shit. Nice, eh? Like I said, bullying was out of control on these units and the screws didn't know half of what went on. Right in the middle of this torture session, in walked the screws and caught them. The victim gave detailed evidence against them, which made matters worse. My mate was hauled before the Governor, lost his parole and got twenty-eight days on top of his sentence. So now, instead of three days left, he had another seven months to do. He was devastated. Well, you would be, wouldn't you, but, as they say, shit happens.

I was due for my parole very shortly now, all my probation reports had been done and I was even told by the Assistant Governor that I had it in the bag and I would be going home in a matter of weeks. Buzzing wasn't in it. I had done nearly eight months and to be perfectly honest I'd had a bellyful.

One night, just before my parole hearing, we were ready to watch the Liverpool v Juventus European Cup game on the telly. It was being played at the Heysel Stadium. What unfolded on the screen was beyond belief. We watched the Liverpool fans storm the Juventus fans and at first thought it was just a bit of fighting, a bit of hooliganism, if you like. Then we realised what was happening and saw that a wall had collapsed and people were being crushed to death. The police and paramedics were carrying dead bodies round the pitch and you could see people receiving heart massage. It was a disaster happening right before our eyes. I couldn't believe what I was watching. A total of thirty-nine fans lost their lives at that game, and it was all down to football hooligans. I went back to my cell that night, thought about what I'd seen – and in truth, wondered whether it would affect my parole. The next day the press and media jumped on it. It was on every news programme for weeks after, and football hooligans were condemned.

My parole hearing came and I had either three weeks left or nine months, a big difference in anybody's book. I walked into the screws' office and they told me to sit down. My heart was racing and I could feel my palms were all clammy. I was shitting myself. The screw started his speech.

"Unfortunately, Paul, you've been knocked back on your parole."

He then started giving me reasons why. I didn't even hear them. He was now just talking shite and the words were not being registered. They were bouncing off me; I was in a daze. I was so disappointed I thought I would fall in a heap. I remember going back to the landing and all thoughts about me going home, which was all I'd thought about for weeks, were now leaving my brain. I couldn't get my head round what I'd heard, and for days I was wounded.

After the mayhem and death that night in Heysel Stadium, hooliganism got so much bad press that the Parole Board had refused my parole to show that they would make a stand against it. So that night's events had cost me my parole. But people say life goes on, and it does, even in jail, so I picked myself up and had to get on with it.

THE BRICK

My first son had been born in the May and was only a couple of months old. My girlfriend had been three months pregnant when I was sentenced, so I was gutted that I had so much time left to do. She was a rock to me when I was inside and actually wrote to me every day, right through my sentence. There were no phones in jail in those days, so letters were our only way of communication, apart from a two-hour visit every fortnight.

A couple of weeks later, I started going to the gym and using weights. I didn't have a clue what to do at first, as it was all new to me, but I soon got the hang of it and actually started to enjoy it. Before long I had been bitten by the bug and soon saw big differences in my body. I was responding to the weights very quickly and was surprised how I was changing. Not only was I a violent football hooligan; now I was becoming a big, violent football hooligan, a good combination in my eyes.

I trained every day for the next few months and tried to keep my nose clean. I was brought before our Wing Officer and asked if I fancied an outside job. Fucking right I do, I thought. When lads were due out in a few months, there were a number of jobs available outside the Centre, and it meant leaving the jail first thing in the morning with a packed lunch, and going into Barnard Castle centre to work at different places. My job was at a place called Witham Hall, a large old building on the High Street. I had to report to the caretaker first thing, and he would give me jobs to do, like setting tables out for the tea dances. There was a café in there as well.

My first morning I picked up my packed lunch from Lee "Oathead" Owens, who worked in the kitchens. He had been a Boro hooligan for years, so we go back a long way. I left the jail about 8.30am and walked the short distance into Barnard Castle. It was a very strange feeling. I was free, but the excitement soon subsided as I knew I had to be back at five o'clock.

When I walked out of the gates in a morning, anybody who had finished their sentence would also come out at the same time as me. As they invariably had money, I quickly caught on to asking them for a couple of quid in order to buy necessities when I got to Barnard Castle. Most lads said, "No problem" and happily handed over cash for my goodies.

The caretaker in Witham Hall was a lad of about twenty-five. He seemed okay and told me he felt sorry for me. He also had a young baby and said he wouldn't like to be away from his baby like I was. I fully exploited his feelings and asked if I could use the phone to call home. "No problem," he said. "Just go in the office and stay on as long as you like." Not one to take advantage, I phoned my girlfriend every day, called the lads up, and just generally abused his good nature. A couple of days later I asked him if he would go to the shop for me, as we weren't allowed in any of the shops. He agreed. It was sweets at first, but after he had been going to the shop for me a couple of times, sweets turned to lager and he got me four cans every day. I explained to him where I was getting the money from and he was happy to do me a favour.

Among my jobs, I served in the café, and when some of the other Boro lads were getting visits in jail the lads who were visiting would come in and give me money. This was doing jail the easy way. I'd also heard rumours before I got my outside job that the local slags from Barnard Castle would visit these places because they knew the lads who had these jobs would be dying for a leg over. Sure enough, I didn't have to wait long. I was behind the counter when this young blonde lass walked in. "Hello," she said, "I'll have a coffee," and fixed me with a smile. Next thing she was at the counter chatting me up. I didn't take much chatting up, and we were soon in the storeroom ripping each other's clothes off. She was wearing stockings, sussies, The full Monty. I couldn't believe my luck. Not only was I using the phone and drinking lager every day, now I was even getting a shag. You couldn't buy a job like that.

Another of the local lasses came in one day and I ended up in the toilets with her. A couple of days later the two of them were in the café arguing over me. Ha, ha! Good girls. I went back to the Centre every night and held my breath while I was getting searched, so the screw wouldn't smell the alcohol. When I went back on the landing the lads used to say I stank of booze. Not bad for being in jail.

Some of the lads visiting other Boro lads in Deerbolt came to the place where I worked and, "Come on, jump in the car and we'll take you home. Fuck the jail." But I knew I was near the end and it would have only meant more time added on and being sent to a secure prison, so I declined their offers. The outside job went on for a couple of months and I fully exploited it until one day, when I had about two months left, they offered me a week in a home somewhere down south. It would mean me leaving the jail, going there to work for a week and then returning to the jail to finish off my sentence. I agreed and was told to go to Darlington on the bus to meet someone for an interview about the placement. While I was on the bus I started thinking and decided I had such a cushy number at Witham Hall I'd be a fool to pack it in. So, when I went for the interview I told them, "No thanks." The woman who interviewed me was a right horrible cow, and she phoned the Custody Centre and said I had totally wasted her time. Half an hour later the screws were there and I was handcuffed, taken back to Deerbolt, and charged with wasting the Governor's time. There goes my job at Witham Hall, I thought.

I went down the block and spent a week there, lost fourteen days' remission and was to be taken back to Durham to finish my sentence. I'd turned twenty-one by now, so I knew I would go on the normal wing, and not the young prisoners' wing. I was fucking mortified. I was used to drinking, using the phone and shagging every day. Now all that was gone. Back to wanking, I suppose.

I arrived in Durham Jail a week later and that pungent, pissy smell hit me again. What a shithole. I spent the next seven days in Durham and was then told I was being moved to Haverigg Prison, on the west coast, near Carlisle, in the middle of nowhere. I only had about twelve weeks to do, so it wasn't that bad. I just had to get on with it. Haverigg was another shithole. Mind you, all old prisons are shitholes and full of the dregs of society. Don't get me wrong, you meet some good lads in jail, but most are just low-life horrible fuckers.

I got a job in Haverigg. It was aptly named Rock Party and entailed filling a flat barrow with as many rocks as you could fit on it, then pulling it half a mile or so to where there was another massive pile of rocks, then emptying the barrow, and so on, and so on, all day long. The lads told me that once all the rocks had been moved from one place to the other, then you had to do exactly the same – only in reverse. A soul-destroying exercise, and it was freezing cold.

I continued to weight-train like mad, right through the rest of my sentence, and when I was released I'd put on a stone and a half of muscle. I was eventually released in March, 1986, after serving sixteen and a half months inside. It wasn't all bad, we had some good laughs, but the big question when I was released was, "Have you learned your lesson?" Had I fuck! Basically, youth custody was one laugh after another. The only downside was you were away from home and at the time I was bang into going to the football matches with the lads, so I missed all that, but I didn't miss much else. Was jail a deterrent? I don't think so. When I received my sentence in 1984, football violence was in the early stages as far as the casual scene goes but was rife when I was released, so I just went straight back to it. I received my sentence for being part of a gang that ambushed a pub full of Barnsley supporters. They weren't innocent bystanders or scarf heads, they were lads just like us who had come to Middlesbrough looking for an off. They just got more than they bargained for.

I look back and think that maybe the slashing of four of their lads was going too far, but what's done is done and I can't change that. One thing's for sure though, it put Middlesbrough on the map as far as football hooliganism goes and we have remained there ever since. I believe the football scene is dying now with all the banning orders. Every mob in the country is getting smaller. Years ago, we always had younger lads coming through to take the older lads' places but that doesn't seem to be the case nowadays. It's also a big risk now being a hoolie, which is why I don't go any more. It was my choice to stop, no-one made the decision for me, I'd just had enough.

But that was in the future. When I left jail, football violence was at its peak, and we'd heard stories of the Boro mob "doing it" all over the country, so I couldn't wait to join them again. I was bigger, stronger, and fitter, and couldn't wait to make my mark.

MAKING ENDS MEET

I HAD BEEN out of prison about three weeks and I was skint. I had no money, no job and no real prospects. At the time, looking back, I didn't really want a job. I just needed a good way to make money to pay for my nights out and away days with the Boro lads. I came up with the answer – shoplifting. I had been talking to one of my old mates, a well-known shoplifter, so we got our heads together and decided to team up to make a couple of quid. He was already experienced in this field and knew the score, but with my brass neck and loads of bottle, we made a formidable team.

I was no stranger to shoplifting but together we took it to greater heights. We would hire cars for the week and go all over the country, relieving shops of their goods and then selling them at night to the lads in our local pub. Very soon word had got around that if you wanted anything half-price, you came and saw us, as we were the lads to get it for you.

In those days, very few shops had cameras or electronic tags, so it was a piece of piss, the phrase "taking candy from a baby" was appropriate as we just took what we wanted. The lads from the pub would have lists for us for the next day's outing. You name it, it was stolen. The best sellers at the time were jeans, perfume, after shave, spirits and clothes, but anything else on the list was not a problem. Nine times out of ten we got it. How I saw it, we were stealing from the rich and selling it to the poor, modern day Robin Hoods, only we never wore green tights, or ever fucked Maid Marion.

A favourite trick was to walk into a clothing shop with an empty Hoover box pretending you were carrying a new Hoover, then select about ten pairs of jeans and, bam, in the box they went. Often the sales assistant would open the door for us on the way out as if we were carrying a heavy vacuum cleaner. Don't laugh, it's not their fault. We exploited no tags and no CCTV to the hilt. We wouldn't work anywhere near where we lived, it was always away from home so that we wouldn't be recognised. Once we'd hit a shop with the Hoover box, it was straight back to the car and away to the next town or city to do the same again. Sometimes we'd hit a large chemist and be away with ten or fifteen bottles of expensive aftershave in one go. With no cameras it was a doddle. We had any number of trolley dashes all over the country and thought it was hilarious. We were making good money and this was funding my football away matches and my nights out.

We used to turn up at the pub in a car packed with goodies and within minutes the car would be empty and our wallets would be full. One particular bloke with loads of money bought any amount of stuff off us, all for half price. One day we'd been to an ex-catalogue shop and they had quite a few pairs of leather trousers at £49.99 a pair, so we robbed ten of them. We told him they were from a designer shop and £100 a pair. He pulled out a wad of notes and bought them all for £50 each. We left his house and cracked up laughing. If he'd got off his arse and gone to the same shop he'd have got them a penny a pair cheaper, legally. Never mind, he thought he was getting a good deal and we were quids in.

Shoplifting was work to us and we thoroughly enjoyed our jobs, but it all came to an abrupt end when we were on our way home one day with a car full of swag and decided to stop at a small village just outside York. We went into a local supermarket, bought something daft and I robbed 200 fags from behind the till. Not thinking we'd been seen, we casually walked out of the shop and back towards the car. Suddenly we could hear footsteps from behind. We'd been seen all right, and now were being pursued by two male staff.

"Just a minute lads," they said. "Can you come back to the shop with us"?

"Go fuck yourselves," came the reply, and we carried on walking.

We thought we'd better not go back to the car as they would get the registration number, so we walked past it. By this time the women in the shop had alerted everybody to this crime of the century in their small village, and half the village was out. We legged it and hid inside a bin cupboard and waited. Fifteen minutes later, we heard sirens. I don't know what they would have done if we'd have killed someone. We made our move and ran across some fields, but halfway across two police cars came screaming to the edge with their lights flashing and there must have been twenty or so villagers with dogs. It is funny as fuck now, but it wasn't at the time.

One of the villagers shouted, "Stop, or I'll let the dog go."

Did we stop? Did we fuck. Did he let the dog go? You bet. A big half- Alsatian, half-bear came running across the field, barking like the Hound of the Baskervilles, straight at us. It ran straight up to my mate, who was shitting himself. The dog lurched forward and my mate screamed, "Argh, argh," as if he was in extreme pain. The dog promptly licked his hand. I was bad laughing. I thought we'd get our arses bitten off, not licked to death.

They closed in and we were arrested. They also found the car with all our swag in it. The villager who let the dog go was eventually promoted to village idiot, or so I heard. We were taken to York Police Station and charged with organised shoplifting. What makes me laugh is that during interview they always ask you the same question: "Have you ever done this before?" Yeah, course I have officer, I do it for a living, didn't you know? Doh!

We were sentenced to three months inside. I'd only been out six months and was back in again. We were taken to Hull Prison and, to be perfectly honest, it was just the same as Durham, that same piss-vomit smell, and everything was as old as the hills. Not a nice place. We spent a week there, which wasn't bad, before being relocated to Rudgate Open Prison. It had dormitories with six beds in them, you could come and go as you pleased all over the prison and there was only a six-foot wire fence all the way round it. Being so lax, you hardly ever saw the screws, so when people were getting visits their visitors would leave fags, vodka, whiskey, blow, anything, so every weekend was party night. People were falling all over blind drunk. You'd think that this could never go on in a prison, but those of you who were there in the Eighties know what I'm talking about.

Some lads went to visit a mate of mine in there one night. They took trays of cans, climbed over the fence and went into the dormitory for a party. They had a camera with them and took pictures inside the dorm. I've seen the pictures and it doesn't shock me, parties were a regular thing in Rudgate. We spent six weeks there and were finally released, with excellent timing, just before the Darlington versus Middlesbrough match, which was going to be a cracker.

I'd continued weight training after getting out of Deerbolt and somebody introduced me to steroids, which I jumped at straight away. I was amazed how my body responded. I'd always taken drugs of some sort, so steroids were just a natural progression, and I loved them. I put a couple of stones on in a matter of months, and was now starting to put on a lot of size. I wasn't that skinny football hooligan any more. I was now becoming a big fucker and people were starting to take notice. I loved it, and training became second nature. I was now eating the right foods as well, so my gains were coming quicker than I'd expected and, before long, I was just under seventeen stones.

DARLINGTON

AS ANYBODY WHO has played Darlington knows, the little market town in the North East yields a large mob of soccer hooligans. In those days their main mob was the Banktop 200, and we knew they'd be well up for it when we played at their place on 8 November, 1986, having been relegated to Division Three the previous season. We expected a massive show and they didn't let us down. We had been talking about this game for ages but weren't sure of the best way for us to converge on Darlo. We knew that if we went in one large mob the police would be on to us straight away, so it was agreed that we'd go in smaller mobs and meet up in the town centre.

Forty of us arrived in Darlo by train around 11.30am. We were with a lad from Darlo who used to come with us to the Boro games and said he'd show us where to go and get a drink, out of the way from the police. We wanted to get out of the way until the rest of our mob arrived. We didn't know it, but he was setting us up.

We walked into the town centre expecting a show from Darlo straight away but nothing happened. We had walked a short distance, heading out of town, when I noticed two lads sitting on a wall outside a social club. When we got closer they stood up and casually walked inside. Nobody thought anything of it until the main doors to the club burst open and around 200 Darlo lads came steaming out. They threw glasses at us, pool balls, fire extinguishers, everything. We clumped together in a tight unit and then they charged. I thought we'd be fucked straight away, but most of our mob were good lads and we ran straight at them. I think they were quite surprised at how game we were because, in all honesty, we weren't doing badly.

I then got whacked with a fire extinguisher that put me on my arse, and I found myself getting surrounded. I was scrambling to my feet when one of Darlos lads kicked me in the chest and the blow lifted me straight back onto my feet (cheers, mate). I traded punches with anyone in front of me, as did all our lads, but it looked like we were about to be done in. Then the police arrived and the Darlo lads all ran back into the club.

The police sent us into the town centre where, by this time more Boro lads had arrived, and we quickly took it over. Sirens were wailing everywhere and fighting between rival fans was moving from pub to pub. There were running battles in all the side streets. I don't think the police knew what had hit them. To put it mildly, they were stretched.

About half an hour before kick off we made our way to the ground and into the side terrace, right next to where all their lads were standing. Boro severely outnumbered Darlo. About five minutes before kick-off, there was a small skirmish in the Darlo end, which was the signal for hundreds of Boro fans to invade the pitch and go straight at the Darlo lads. They responded by coming on to the pitch and the mass brawl that took place was like the Wild West. Every man and his dog was fighting on the pitch. I doubt they've seen anything like this before or since. The fighting went on for around five minutes, and it took a lot longer for the police to restore order, so the kick-off was delayed. During the match there were a further two pitch invasions by the Boro fans and to say it was a mad day would be an understatement.

A total of eighty-eight people were arrested on the day and five were stabbed. Of those stabbed, none made a complaint. Funny that, isn't it?

The local newspaper reported the carnage:

> Soccer thugs held a town under siege using military-style battle plans, police revealed today.
>
> Organised gangs fought running street battles in Darlington during a wanton orgy of violence.
>
> Hundreds of terrified shoppers – including peace poppy sellers – fled as local louts clashed with yobs following the Boro.
>
> Hooligans from the Redcar Casuals, Northallerton Blues, Darlington's Bank Top 200 and Under Fives armed themselves with bleach, Stanley knives and pool balls before Saturdays's North-east derby.
>
> Two policemen were injured and five youths stabbed in an afternoon of terror planned as far back as last season.
>
> On the day the Boro were relegated to Division Three, its central core of hooligans were chanting, "See you at Darlington."

The following account is by a long-time friend of mine from Darlington. Even though he followed Middlesbrough in the early Eighties, that all changed when Boro were drawn against Darlo in the third round of the F.A. Cup. He had to make a decision then and he made it – to follow his home team into

battle against lads he had stood side by side with up and down the country. He wishes to remain anonymous.

If you were to ask any Darlington lad what was the biggest game, as far as hooliganism goes, in the Eighties, every one of them would say Middlesbrough. Middlesbrough is only fourteen miles from Darlo, but at the time it might as well have been a million miles away as far as hooliganism goes. We were only a small mob of up and coming hooligans but were soon to become a mob to be reckoned with. Boro's mob at the time were known as "The Boys" or "The Joeys" and had established a reputation in the early part of the decade as a mob of casuals to be feared.

In 1982, Darlo played Sheffield United in United's last game of the season in what was their celebration game because they had been promoted. Ten thousand Sheffield United fans came to Darlo but the party was crashed by a mob of around sixty Boro casuals. The few Darlo casuals around at the time teamed up with Boro, and running battles were fought throughout the town. This day was the first of many when some of the Darlo casuals, including myself, teamed up with Boro. In the early days, trips to Chelsea, Fulham, Charlton, Hull, Arsenal and Leeds were too much of an incentive because at the time Darlo were doing pretty shit and there was very little (if any) trouble with Darlo. However, things soon changed. Darlo went from having a hardcore of maybe thirty casuals to around two to three hundred by the 1984/1985 season. Some of the older lads were splitting their time between Darlo and Boro. Some may frown on this but lads like me had followed Boro since the Jack Charlton days of the 1970s and had an active interest in how the team did. Others were there for the violence and you were always guaranteed that with Boro.

We had made some good mates among the Boro lads and went with them to the Northern Soul all-nighters. In the mid-Eighties the Bank Top 200 was born, named after the train station in town. We created a good reputation for ourselves with trips away to the likes of Port Vale, Stockport, and Blackpool. Most of the Fourth Division teams saw good turnouts away, and at home we felt invincible.

The team managed to reach the third round of the FA Cup and we were drawn away to Middlesbrough. I couldn't believe it. After all the years of following them, Darlo draw them in the fucking Cup. There was no choice to be made. I loved the "offs" with the Boro mob all over the country but I was a Darlo lad, born and bred, and it will always be my hometown. After all, I was an original member of the Bank Top 200 and proud of it, so it had to be done. I was to go to Ayresome Park against the mighty Boro as the enemy.

This was our biggest test by far. We had never come up against a mob like this before and we knew we would have to make a good show. We knew we would take good numbers to Boro – even the older lads came out of retirement for this one. We travelled by bus and taxi through to Stockton, a town just four miles from Middlesbrough, and met at the Number Nine pub at the Norton Road end of the town. We had a good set of lads with us and the young 'uns, or Under Fives as they were called, were mooching about looking for anyone who fancied it. They found it with one of Boro's main lads, who lived in Stockton. He had armed himself with an iron bar and a couple of our lads were on the receiving end of it. It was only a brief scuffle but news soon filtered back to us. When we went to investigate, the small mob of Boro that had been there were gone. We made our way to Thornaby train station for the short ride into Middlesbrough centre. Whilst we were waiting for the train we had the worlds biggest snowball fight with each other.

We arrived at Middlesbrough station and started the long, familiar walk up Linthorpe Road to Ayresome Park. It was a bit strange because this time I was the enemy. Nothing happened on Linthorpe Road, to my surprise, but as we got to the Clive Road end of Ayresome Park a few Boro lads decided to mount an attack on us. A lad came straight at me and I managed to gouge him right in the eye. It went off briefly before the Old Bill came in swiftly and got between us.

When we entered the Clive Road end we found a spot at the top right next to the seats, which was at the time a favourite haunt of the Boro lads. A small pocket of Boro had infiltrated our end and as we made our way to get at them the Old Bill sussed it and ejected them. The match, attended by 5,000 Darlo, was a draw so we were rubbing our hands at the thought of the replay at our place.

On match day the following week, we were disorganised. We had a major group at the pubs on Bank Top with other small pockets of lads dotted around the town. In the ground itself there was no segregation as such, so the well-organised Boro mob just ran round the terracing, getting stuck in all over the ground. After the game a battle that would become infamous took place on the cricket pitch outside the ground, with both mobs meeting head-on. The fight went on for quite some time, with both mobs giving as good as each other until the Old Bill restored order.

The following season saw both Middlesbrough and Darlington clash again, this time in a Third Division league game. Both sets of fans waged war on each other from early morning until late in the day. On this particular day Darlo's Bank Top 200 met at 10am outside the Engineers' Club in the Northgate area of town instead of the usual Market Square pubs. This would ensure that we would be already mobbed up when we entered the town centre, where the masses of Boro would be. Numbers steadily grew to around two or three hundred and when the club opened at 11am we piled inside, leaving a couple of Under Fives outside to keep an eye on the road for any Boro.

Around twelve o'clock a shout went up that a Boro mob was coming. We raced outside and went straight at the Boro mob, which only numbered about forty. They had come into the town this way led, funnily enough, by a Darlo lad who had advised them that this route would help them avoid the police. But we were waiting. We totally took them by surprise and they backed off into the middle of the road, with some of them taking a severe kicking. Paul Debrick was in this small mob of Boro and he agrees that they were well outnumbered and well ambushed on this occasion.

The police arrived so we made good our escape through North Lodge Park and through the subway into town. I'll never forget the sight as the full mob of Darlo's Bank Top 200 ran through the subway with the police trying to force us back. One of the Old Bill was knocked to the ground and sparked out. Incidentally, one of our lads received a hefty jail sentence for this even though it was not him who floored the copper.

By the time we reached the town it was a different story. Boro had regrouped and had their full mob out in force and we had been split into two smaller mobs. I was with a group of about thirty or forty lads who I could count on to stand, so we went straight at the Boro mob. I had taken up Thai boxing and I can remember one of the lads saying to me that he wanted to see some of my moves. As I came at a Boro lad I threw a punch and missed by a mile. As I regained my balance I tried to do a roundhouse kick to his head, lost my balance and ended up on my arse with Boro kicks and punches being rained down on my head. I made a right arse of myself. There were offs happening all over the town centre as small pockets of Boro met small mobs of Darlo. It was mental; I've never seen it so bad.

We made our way up to High Row to another favourite pub, The George, and a massive Boro mob marched towards us. This was one of those moments of exhilaration and fear both at the same time. Boro's mob charged straight at us and we turned to face them. As we clashed, Saturday shoppers scattered all over the place as lads were going for it in the middle of the road. One unfortunate shopper had her pram with her baby in it knocked over. It was an unfortunate incident, I know, as no one likes to see innocent bystanders hurt. The funny thing is, the baby in the pram grew up to become one of Darlington's top youths, so he can say he started young. One of our main faces received six months in jail for his part in the brawl. Even before the kick-off, sixty-nine people were arrested. We made our way to the Three Crowns pub to get out of the way, as the police were looking for those involved in the High Row incident.

During the game there was more violence with the Boro mob kicking off in every section of the ground. All in all this was one of the best days we have had on the hooligan calendar. Ask any Boro lad there that day and he'll tell you Darlo made a good show against one of the top mobs in the country.

STAG NIGHTS, BIRTHDAYS, ANY EXCUSE

IN THE LATE EIGHTIES I was living back in Hemlington. The girl I was with had bought a house and I had returned to my roots. I knew all the Hemlington lads, some of them went to the matches and some didn't, but one thing we all had in common was our love of a ruck. We used any excuse to plan trips away, whether it was a stag night, a birthday, or if someone's budgie had been christened. The occasion didn't matter really, all that mattered was that we had an excuse to get to another town and, to be honest, go mental. We planned these trips weeks in advance and looked forward to them like away matches. Every trip had one thing in common: violence. And we loved it.

We arranged a trip to Scarborough one Saturday night for one of the lads' birthdays. Everyone was going to be there. When the day arrived we met in the Smithy pub in Coulby Newham and waited for the coach. We always went drinking in the early afternoon and we were half tanked up before we even set off. One of the lads came round with a big bag of speed and everyone dipped their fingers in it and licked them clean. You could never have a good day out without the three main ingredients – drink, drugs and violence – and we did them all to excess.

By the time the coach came at around four o'clock, everyone was whizzing off their tits and all anybody could talk about was what was going to happen in Scarborough. Every time we went away we promised each other we would just have a quiet drink and a laugh, but we were kidding ourselves, it always ended up in a mass brawl. Most of the time it wasn't us who caused it, but wherever we went the locals took a dislike to us and would get mobbed up and attack us. Not that we were bothered, we'd take on all comers. Looking back, I'm surprised we got away with what we did.

We boarded the coach with all the bottles, cans and spirits you could wish for and pissed about all the way to Scarborough. I can't remember how many times we stopped for a piss stop when all forty drunken louts got off the bus and pissed all over the road. Not a nice sight, I would imagine, but at the time no one gave a fuck. We arrived in Scarborough just before six o'clock and hit the first pub we came to. Everyone was fucking about and just being generally obnoxious. I don't think the manager quite knew what to do, but what could he do, apart from hope for the best?

Someone said the comedian, Roy "Chubby" Brown, who comes from our neck of the woods, was appearing at the Futurist Theatre that night, so it was agreed that we would all go, as it would be a laugh. We arrived at the theatre and everyone was trying to act dead sensible so as not to get turned away. They told us we had to sit downstairs in the stalls but we thought different and decided to sit on our own at the front of the balcony. Lads were skinning up joints and drinking cans. We must have been a nightmare.

A few minutes passed and two security lads came upstairs and walked across to us.

"Look lads," one of them said, "you have to go and sit downstairs."

All the lads just sat and looked at them, until one said, "Here mate, fuck off."

The other security lad, a big fella who up until now had been silent, walked over. I thought he was going to kick off with us, then in the campest voice you could imagine, he said, "You fuck off." Everyone cracked up laughing; we couldn't believe what had just come out of his mouth. He stood there with his mate, and I honestly think he didn't know what we were laughing at. Every time he spoke we just laughed more, until in the end he said, "Look, you can all stay up here, but only if you behave yourselves." We all nodded, and said, "Okay mate. We'll behave, just leave us and we'll be alright." They left us and went back downstairs. Big mistake. One of the lads at the front stood up and pissed into the crowd directly below us. They must have thought the roof was leaking.

This time around half a dozen security men came back and demanded to know who had thrown the drink.

"No one," we all said. Well, we weren't lying, were we?

"Any more and you are all out."

"Yeah, okay lads, now fuck off again."

They did, only this time the camp one didn't speak. This had all happened even before Brown had come onto the stage, it was still only around 7.30. Eventually, he appeared and what an act. If you've ever seen him live on stage, you know what I'm talking about, if you haven't, then go, you won't be disappointed.

A lot of friendly banter went on between Chubby and ourselves. He's a Boro lad as well, so we had a lot of time for him, and still have. He sent me a birthday card for my fortieth. On the cover is a picture of Chubby shagging Bin Laden up the arse. When you open the card it says, "Told you he'd be fucked by Christmas." Ha, ha! Funny man!

We left the theatre at around nine o'clock, wanting some fun. We walked into the first pub, which was quite busy, and got a drink. We were talking and generally fucking about, just having a good time really. We saw some local lads giving us the eye but thought nothing of it. A short while later, one of the local lads said something to one of ours and, you guessed it, he was swiftly right-handed and then he and his entourage were attacked and beaten senseless. Most times when you're out with a gang of lads, even when you're not looking for trouble, when you're in a strange town it finds you, and it found us every time.

We went to another couple of pubs, had several more drinks and it was relatively peaceful. We were just enjoying ourselves. We decided to go to the local nightclub and as we were walking we noticed the locals hanging about in small groups. We weren't sure when it would happen, but it was only a matter of time. We walked into the club but nobody paid, we just walked up the stairs and up to the bar. I think the doorman decided to keep quiet. It wasn't very busy at this time, with just a few people scattered around having drinks. I made a comment to my brother, Mark, that there would be trouble later as the locals were now filling the club, and I could see we were getting the eye again. Word had obviously spread about what we'd done earlier, and they wanted revenge. I mean, who were we to come into their town and take the piss? They weren't going to let us get away with it, at least that's what they thought.

By about midnight most of us were standing on the edge of the dance floor. The bar area was slightly raised with five or six steps up to that level. A large mob of local lads were stood there, and it was inevitable that there was going to be an off. A few minutes passed and their mob was getting larger, and I was now looking in their direction. Out of the corner of my eye I could see my brother standing behind these lads, looking at us and laughing. Obviously, the locals didn't know he was with us, as no-one even batted an eyelid, and then it happened. Mark grabbed two lads, one under each arm, and ran down the stairs towards us with both lads in a headlock. Crash! He ran both the lads straight into a pillar, head first, and they were both out on the floor.

The whole club erupted. They came at us down the stairs, throwing punches and kicks, and everyone went metal. We attacked them and the whole dance floor was engulfed in lads fighting. Lasses were screaming and running in every direction, trying to flee the fighting. We all went forward and whacked the locals all over, lads were laid in heaps on the dance floor, bleeding everywhere. The fighting went on for a few minutes, and they knew we had the upper hand. They backed off and scattered. The few that got caught were savagely beaten. Somebody shouted that we should get out of the club before the police came, so we all marched out and started down the stairs. We were halfway down when what seemed like the whole club came steaming down at us. We turned to confront them and at first they had the upper hand. They backed us off into the street and the doormen joined them, probably because we didn't pay to get in.

We regrouped and attacked again, and punches were traded through the doors from both sides. They panicked when they realised we weren't backing off and tried to run back up the stairs. One of the doormen drop-kicked one of our lads on to the pavement and at that moment one of our lads ran forward and swung a punch. The doorman moved back slightly and the punch missed his face by a fraction. Then everyone realised what had happened. The lad who had thrown the punch was holding a large knife in his hand and had been trying to stab the doorman in the head. One doorman shit himself and ran like fuck, probably to change his undies. We never saw him again. We grabbed the lad with the knife.

"Are you fucking mental," someone asked. "You'd have taken his fucking head off."

He just laughed and said, "I fucking should have."

This was supposed to be a quiet night in Scarborough. The remaining doormen slammed and locked the door, and we walked off. Surprisingly, no police turned up and we ended up at the Kentucky. We were standing in small groups outside, eating our food, when a group of lads came round the corner and wanted to confront us. They were quickly beaten up. When they were backing off they shouted, "We're the Army and we'll be back." Yeah, yeah, we thought. We'd had it with everybody else that night, so we weren't bothered, even if it was the Army, which we didn't think it was anyway.

A short while later, a large open-backed Army vehicle reversed into the road, about 100 yards away from where we were, and about twenty lads jumped out of the back. They were being led by a big barrel-chested bloke with a large 'tache. They started to jog towards us. We couldn't believe our eyes. I think we half expected a tank to come round the corner and start firing at us. When we realised what was happening, everyone just attacked. We ran at them, screaming and shouting, "Fucking come on then." We thought we were in for one hell of a battle when, all of a sudden they turned and ran like fuck. The Army wagon started moving off, and they were all diving in the back shouting, "Wait for me." To any bystander this must have been hilarious.

The police turned up in large numbers and everybody was searched. The doorman from the club had obviously told them that one of us had a knife, but the search was fruitless and no knife was found. They held us there until our bus came and warned us not to come back or we'd be arrested. We were given a police escort right back into Middlesbrough. The police car was directly behind the coach, following us home. One of the lads needed a piss but the driver wouldn't stop, so the lad said, "Well, open the fucking door then, and I'll piss while the bus is moving." The driver did this, and he relieved himself out of the door. All the lads at the back of the bus were screaming laughing, as they watched the piss go all over the police car and they had to put their windscreen wipers on. One by one, all the way home, we took it in turns to piss out of the door, and the police couldn't turn the wipers off all the way back to Middlesbrough. Funny wasn't in it. The car must have stunk of piss by the time we got back.

When we were dropped off we couldn't wait to do it again and we didn't have to wait long as it was another lad's birthday in a couple of weeks and we already had a trip sorted. Look out Bridlington, here we come.

BRIDLINGTON

As usual, we'd been looking forward to our next excursion. We always did. We knew we'd always have a good laugh and a brawl, it was just part of our trips away.

We decided we wanted to get to Bridlington around lunchtime, so we could spend all day drinking: a "black 'un" as we called it. We boarded the bus with loads of drink and, in those days, most of us had loads of whizz (speed) to keep us going through the day and so we'd be able to drink all night. No wonder these trips always ended in trouble. A coach full of young lads, full of drink and drugs, in a strange town where the locals always resent you being there. Any normal person would be put off by this but we looked forward to it even more. In normal groups there would be a couple of particular lads who would start trouble, but on our buses it could be anyone who started it. It was never planned, it would just kick off for the daftest thing and then there would be a mass brawl. Bridlington was no different to any other trip. We all knew by the end of the night there'd be the one thing in common with all the others: there'd be trouble.

When we arrived in Bridlington just after lunchtime most of us were buzzing with excitement (and probably whizz). The first pub we found was pretty quiet, well until we got there, anyway.

THE BRICK

We all ordered drinks and just sat, having a laugh and generally pissing about. A couple of local lads told us that we wouldn't get in the nightclub as we were in a large mob. We thought nothing of it and said we'd stay pretty quiet so we wouldn't spoil our chances of getting in, and we planned to split up into small groups and go to the club separately. It's funny how plans don't always work out.

We went into a couple more pubs and it was a generally quiet afternoon. As the day went on, though, we were getting steadily more rowdy, like you do when you're a coach full of loons. We went into another bar, quite large, with a back room with a pool table and one of those kids' rides where you put in 20p and it rocks backwards and forwards. We took our drinks in there and some lads played pool. A few had been to the shops to do a bit of robbing and a roar of laughter went up when they walked in the back room with an array of different hats and loads of teddy bears. Teddy bears? There was probably nothing else to nick. People were getting whacked with teddies, which were thrown all over the place. All the lads were getting a bit mental by this time and it must have been a landlord's nightmare. What do you do when forty lads are throwing teddies and getting out of hand?

One of the lads got on to the little kiddies' ride, which was a giant squirrel, put money in it, and was rocking back and forth. What happened next had me cracked up laughing. Someone came up behind him and tipped the whole ride upside down with him under it, but the ride kept going while he was underneath, so it was now on top of him, rocking up and down. It looked like he was being fucked by a huge, plastic squirrel. He shouted, "Get it off me," but all the lads did was bounce teddy bears off his head. Funny as fuck. When he eventually got out from under it he saw the funny side even though he was known as Squirrel Fucker for the rest of the day.

As the drink and whizz-fuelled rowdiness continued, some of the lads continued to play pool. To say the game wasn't being taken seriously was an understatement. Every time one of the lads was about to take a shot, a teddy bear bounced off his head or the table and knocked the balls all over the place. The lads who were playing protested but it just got worse until, in the end, the teddies were used as balls and fired all over the table.

Someone came back from the bar and said that the landlord was on the phone to the police, so we decided to make a sharp exit. We piled out of the back into the beer garden, which was surrounded by a large, wooden fence with a locked gate. Some of the lads climbed over the fence and one seemed to go straight through it. Anyway, everyone managed to get out but the fence was a picture. It looked like something from a cartoon, where the characters had run through a wall and their body shapes were the holes. It was comical, though not if you had to pay for the fence.

When we went back to the main drag, we noticed that most of the pubs had quite a few lads on the doors. Obviously, word had spread that we were in town and they didn't want us in their premises carrying on like we had been. It was also clear that the locals knew we were there as well, and it would soon turn ugly, it always did. We went in another couple of bars and decided to quieten down a bit, after all, we wanted to get into the nightclub.

When it was time, we split up into twos and threes and decided to walk to the club, which was on the main road on the sea front, amongst some amusement arcades. Across the road was a wide promenade with benches all along it, and cars were parked along the prom. About half a dozen of our lads got into the club, but the rest of us were recognised and refused. We sat on the benches across the road wondering what to do, as all the other bars were now shut.

THE BRICK

We'd been there about half and hour when we heard a commotion coming from the club. The doors opened and the six lads who had got in were being slung out. When they were inside, some of the locals sussed them out as being part of our group and had started fighting with them. They did their best, but six against a full club doesn't weigh up and they were eventually slung out.

While they were telling us what happened, the doors burst open again and what seemed like the whole fucking club came out on to the pavement opposite us. They were obviously about to attack us. We turned and faced them and said, "Come on then." They obliged and came straight across the road. The parked cars along the prom caused us to form into little groups, each packed into the gap between the cars. I thought they would overpower us straight away but, as often happens, you can have 100 lads in a mob but there are maybe only ten or twenty at the front who are game. Everyone on our bus was game, so I think we surprised them.

One skinny twat jumped about in the middle of the road, doing all the Bruce Lee moves, kicking and punching the air and making loads of mad noises. He was obviously the local ninja. As he was in the middle of his routine I ran up and hit him with a cracking right hand straight on the side of his jaw. He didn't see it coming and lifted off his feet and landed like a pile of shit about three or four feet away. That was the end of the ninja.

Out of the corner of my eye I saw a lad running at me. He was cut dead in his tracks when a bin caught him flush in the face. He didn't know what hit him. His mouth and nose were pissing blood, and you could see the horror on his face as he staggered about, probably wondering where the fuck the bin had come from.

In a situation like that, it's them or us, so you get in first. There were bodies lying all over and our lads were in full swing. We were used to this and we enjoyed these occasions. As I was stood in the road, fighting like a loon, I saw a flash and staggered back. The pain was excruciating. I'd been hit with something right on the top of the head. I quickly put my hands up to check the damage but to my surprise there was no blood, just a large lump, but I was okay. I later found out someone had run up and whacked me over the head with a bottle. I don't know whether it was a thick bottle or I've got a hard head, but it didn't break, thank fuck, it just bounced off my head. I wish I could have seen who did it but, unfortunately, or fortunately for him, I didn't.

Some of the locals were in retreat and off up the road and some were still fighting between the cars when the boys in blue turned up. Fortunately, I managed to duck my way past the parked cars and watched what was happening. The police proceeded to whack our lads with batons and locked them up left, right and centre. Not one of the locals got arrested that night but they made sure that the outsiders were going to pay. Out of forty of us, twenty-two were charged with a number of disorder offences. It was in the local paper that they'd caused a riot and each was heavily fined.

I look back on these days out with a great laugh and whenever I meet any of the lads who I haven't seen for a while, we talk about these times over a drink and reminisce about "the good old days". You can't go on like that forever without ending up locked up for a long time and we all moved on. Still, we got away with it for long enough.

SHREWSBURY

The last game of the 1985/86 season was to be played at Shrewsbury and if we lost we'd be relegated. Not that it bothered me in the least but it was another good excuse to kick off if we did get relegated. I was trying to keep a low profile as I'd not long been out of jail for the Barnsley carry on, but I knew as soon as I entered Shrewsbury's ground there would be trouble. Before the game there'd been minor skirmishes in the town and some damage. It was as if our lads already knew we would lose this match, so they were getting the first one in, so to speak. I've never been a Middlesbrough supporter, I think they are shite, but this particular season they were worse than shite; they were, to put it mildly, fucking shite.

We were packed into a terrace behind the goal with a refreshment kiosk at the back of the stand. The atmosphere was electric and soon enough, it happened. Shrewsbury scored and this gave the Boro fans an excuse to start going off. Very shortly Shrewsbury scored again, and that was it. The people in the kiosk at the back had decided to close early because of the stick they were getting and made a sharp exit. However, the Boro lads re-opened it by ripping the wooden shutters clean off, and ransacked the whole stock. The police tried to intervene and for a moment had the upper hand, but the lads broke the shutters up into long sticks and attacked them with the makeshift weapons. The police beat a hasty retreat and had to run on to the side of the pitch to take cover. This left the Boro lads in our enclosure to their own devices, and they climbed on to the perimeter fence and taunted the police with the sticks. Everything was being thrown at the police and there was fuck all they could do to restore order. I thought there would be a full-scale pitch invasion but it didn't happen as there were too many coppers pitch side. It was a funny thing to watch the coppers ducking and diving to dodge the missiles being thrown at them.

Half time came and in marched massive numbers of riot police, straight to our end. A small battle started with them but they were too mob-handed, and eventually order was restored. People were getting nicked everywhere and our local paper later had pictures like a rogues' gallery of people who had been involved in the trouble. Several were jailed for the incident at Shrewsbury and many more had serious fines shoved up their arses. A small town like Shrewsbury didn't know what had hit it. They even kept the home fans locked in the ground at the final whistle and let our 4,000 loons onto the street to cause havoc and wanton destruction. I'm not a great believer in smashing things up, I'd rather give someone a crack, and I'm ashamed to say Boro wrecked Shrewsbury that day. It's not something to be proud of but, hey, at least we're not from Leeds.

BLUE HALF OF
MANCHESTER

I always regarded Manchester City as one of the top firms in the country. They had the numbers, they were always up for it and we got trouble whenever we went to Maine Road. One particular Saturday in the mid 1990s, everybody turned out and the train station was buzzing early in the morning. Everybody had bags full of cans and copious amounts of cocaine. About ten minutes into the journey we had our first can and our first line, not a breakfast Kellogg's would recommend but breakfast all the same.

About 150 of us, all charged up on alcohol and cocaine, arrived at Manchester Piccadilly and came out of the main entrance around 11am. As usual, we arrived on away turf early to give ourselves more opportunities. We walked down the concourse on to the main street and braced ourselves for the attack from Man City, but it never came. Imagine 150 lads bouncing down the road, fully charged, ready for it and it doesn't happen. Disappointment wasn't in it.

We quickly found a pub, went in for a drink and waited. Very shortly the police arrived in large numbers and surrounded the pub. I thought we'd blown our chance, and I didn't think we would get an off that day, but I was wrong. The same day, fifty Hibs casuals also arrived in Manchester on their way to Blackpool for a stag night. They knew several of our lads and had pre-arranged to come into Manchester because they knew there was fun to be had.

We eventually got escorted to the football ground by the police, who kept us in a tight group so we had no chance of escaping and doing what we came for. When we finally got to the ground they herded us in and we sat and watched the game.

Just before the end, it was arranged that we would meet at the main exit so that we would all be together. As we left the ground there must have been some mix-up because 120 of our lads came out and turned left, and about thirty others, including me, turned right. Before we realised what had happened it was too late and we were on our own in the middle of Moss Side where half the city wanted to kill us. It was not for the faint hearted.

We walked a couple of hundred yards up the road and on to a side street which joined the main road at the top. Our small mob included about fifteen good lads with the rest of the number made up by younger lads. I thought to myself, if these young lads want to be game, now is the time to show it. As we approached a T-junction there were City lads everywhere we looked. Adrenalin took over and I was hyper. I turned and told everyone to keep it tight, stay together. This was no time for anybody to lose their bottle. They came straight at us from across the road. This is it, I thought, I am going to that big terrace in the sky.

As the first few approached us, I hit the first one with a left hook and the second with a right. I continued throwing punches like they were going out of fashion and was surprised how easily they were going down. It was good fun. The other lads with me were all doing the same and I was quite pleased with how we were doing. Suddenly, the whole road seemed to attack us. It was like

Custer's Last Stand. Then, two police vans on the way to sort out the trouble crashed into each other and that diverted everybody's attention. Seconds later the road was swarming with police. Thank fuck, I thought. We'd have been killed.

Their mob walked down the main road towards the city centre and we were chased back down the street we had just come up. We ran down to the bottom of the road, turned left and ran straight back up the other street, back towards their mob. They must have thought we were mental. We were just about to have it with them again when the police swarmed us and held us against the wall.

"Are you fucking right in the head?" one copper said to me. "There's only thirty of you lot and half of Manchester's on that road."

No, I'm not right in the head, I thought. Fucking Ted Loon, me, mate.

We were escorted back to the station and up to 400 Man City lads followed us all the way. When we rejoined our main mob at the station we learned that they had just had it with another firm of Man City lads. They must have had some mob out for us. I also learned that in the same street the Hibs lads made a show and wanted to join with our lads but ours attacked them, so there were three mobs in one street, all kicking off. The police didn't know what was going on.

We have had some good days in Manchester. Another time we went there we took the same numbers and again arrived in Piccadilly early doors. This time there was no police presence to speak of so we went into the city centre. We went into the first boozer we found and decided to stay there for a few hours. What a firm we had, 150-strong, every top lad there. I knew that if it did go off it was going to be one hell of a battle.

We walked some distance with no coppers in sight. It was only a matter of time before we found them or they found us and we were going to get what we had come for. We arrived at a large grassed area with a pub across the green and half a dozen lads outside. They saw us coming and started to get very excited, jumping about, and then it happened. The doors of the pub burst open and seventy or eighty lads came running towards us, shouting, "Come on Boro." Our mob ran straight at them like wild animals moving in for the kill. I was quite surprised really because the Man City mob stopped and I don't think they knew quite what to do. As we closed in on them most started running back towards the pub. Some of their lads were shouting, "Stand, stand," but to no avail. They were well and truly on their toes. There must have only been about fifteen who didn't run and they were quickly engulfed in kicks and punches. Some of those who couldn't get back into the pub quick enough jumped on a wall and on to the roof to get away from our mob. Shitbags. We eventually got escorted to the ground. We thought after the game we would have some more of the same but the police saw to it that we didn't.

Good mob, Man City. Respect where it's due, you always turned out for us.

EVERTON

Everton's reputation speaks for itself. The blue half of Liverpool were always a formidable mob. Whether we played them at home or at Goodison Park, they always turned out and were always game as fuck. I've lost count how many times I've been to Goodison Park over the years but every trip had one thing in common, you got what you went for, trouble. I always felt that Everton were pretty similar to ourselves, loved the element of surprise, always came early, and loved an off.

Andy Nichols' book, *Scally* is one of the best football hooligan books available. What's good about it and what makes it better than the rest, is that he tells it like it is, no bullshit. When he writes about Boro in his book and mentions the offs with us, I know he's not talking shite, because I was there at them all; from the time outside the Yankee Bar and the Crown, to Boxing Day, I was there. Our accounts of what happened might differ slightly in terms of numbers and so on, but the facts are true.

Our history goes back a long way with the Blues and we've had some memorable battles with them. Every time we play them it's talked about for weeks beforehand. I wish we could have played them every other week, that would have been fun.

One time in the Nineties we took quite a tasty mob down

there. We'd walked about before the game expecting Everton to make a show but, disappointingly, they didn't, apart from a few lads just before kick-off. With no chew before the game, we walked around Goodison like we owned the place. Every one of our lads was up for it, so when the Blues didn't show I thought they'd lost their way a bit and obviously weren't up for it. How wrong I was. A couple of their lads told us to go to through Stanley Park to the Arkle pub after the game, and that's where we'd get it. Nice one, I thought, and couldn't wait for the game to finish.

We left Goodison Park. We had the numbers, had the top lads, and I expected it to go off big time. We'd managed to shake off the police and everyone was ready. Walking through Stanley Park, I told our lads to be alert. I expected an ambush but it never came. We got to the Arkle, went in and ordered drinks. Our spotters were outside, waiting for Everton to show, and I couldn't understand why they didn't. Some time had passed and people thought it was a no-show, so some of our lads started to do one. When a couple of lads who were in a car offered me a lift home, I accepted and we set off. I was bitterly disappointed. The times I'd been to Everton and we'd always got it, and this time we got nothing.

We'd been in the car about an hour when I received a phone call from one of our lads who had stayed in the Arkle. I was gob-smacked at what I was listening to. Just after I left the pub two of Everton's lads had come in and said to our forty lads who were left, "Stay put, Everton are on their way." The lad who phoned me told me they thought they were full of shit, so they didn't bother to ring us. We must have only been gone about five minutes before, and could have easily been back at the Arkle, but it wasn't to be.

He explained to me that the two lads had said to ours, "If you want it, follow us." Foolishly, they did, straight into an ambush. A short way down the road the Everton mob met them head on. By all accounts our lads were doing quite well, probably because they'd picked up fence posts and rocks on the way. The fighting went on for some time and some of the Boro lads received bad injuries. One of my mates was slashed across the neck and needed stitches to the wound. Everton's mob came out on top on this occasion. I was pissed off, to say the least. If only I'd have stayed a while longer, I'd have been there for the lads, but life is full of "if onlys". Well done Everton; you won the battle but the war was far from over.

We were to get our revenge on Boxing Day when we played them at the Riverside Stadium. They'd been told to come to the Wicker's World pub, and to get there early doors. Incidentally, I was head doorman at the Wicker's at the time, so I knew I'd be there, which was convenient. We'd all planned to be in town as early as we could so we wouldn't be surprised. We wanted revenge and we wanted it pretty bad. What happened to our lads at Everton was a kick in the balls to us, so Boxing Day was payback time. Forget goodwill to all men and all that shite, they were getting it, no matter what. Christmas Day came and all I could think about was the next day. I phoned the lads up and instead of, "All the best, mate," we just talked about what was going to go off the following day.

When Boxing Day finally came I arrived for work at the pub at 11am. Just up the road was the Ayresome Park pub and within half-an-hour it was full to the rafters with every top lad we had. I remember walking in there to see my brother Mark, who was working the door, and I was over the moon that everyone had kept their word and was in town early. Everyone inside the two pubs kept a low profile so as not to get sussed by our Intelligence Unit, and it worked a treat; there wasn't a copper in sight. Now all we needed was Everton to show and it would be payback time.

THE BRICK

I returned to Wicker's World and we sat talking about the usual shite you talk about on Boxing day, how many pairs of socks you got for Christmas from your auntie and so on. I'd just returned from the toilets, where I'd had a chocca line of coke to get me charged up, when one of our lads came bursting through the door.

"They're here, they're here."

At first I thought it was a wind-up, but to my delight I could see around fifty lads outside coming straight for the door. Nice one, I thought. They'd made a show and were now in our town, on our soil, and wanting it. Did we oblige? You bet we did. There were only a handful of us in the pub at the time, but we headed straight for the door. Glasses flew over my head and out on to the street. One of the Everton's lads ran forward and attempted to spray the door with CS gas. I don't know whether the clown was cockeyed or not, but he missed the door and it went up the wall outside.

There was a slight standoff for a few seconds while a ginger twat called me on. What happened next was brilliant. Someone in the other pub shouted what was going on, the doors burst open and the road quickly filled with our mob. Everton's attention was diverted by this and, in a split second I saw my chance. "Smack". I connected with a corker of a right hand, and the ginger cunt fell backwards into the road. I followed up with a penalty kick to his head for good measure.

I could see some of them were carrying blades, which just made me go off it and when the other lads with me in the pub came steaming out, I shouted, "These fuckers are tooled up." All thoughts of what had happened at Goodison came flooding back to me and all I wanted to do was as much damage in as short a time as I possibly could.

By now our entire mob was bearing down on Everton and, to give them their due, they stood their ground and under the circumstances were game on. Fighting was now taking place on both sides of the road. It didn't matter where you looked, it was going off. There wasn't a copper in sight, a perfect opportunity for revenge. I knew this was going to be good. Across the road I could see around ten Everton who'd split off and were fronting some of our lads. I ran straight across at them and they didn't see me coming from the side. I drop-kicked the nearest one, who flew into a couple of their lads and they went down like skittles. Those who fell were quickly engulfed by kicks and punches. The Boro mob were hellbent on revenge that day; we wanted to show Everton we hadn't lost it. I loved every minute.

As I was fighting under the bridge, I turned and saw a big lad wearing a Tommy Hilfiger top, running fast. He had a yellow craft knife in his hand and it looked like he'd just cut someone. I just saw red and stopped him dead in his tracks with a right hand and he fell like a bust lift. You Scouse bastard, I thought, you're getting it. I rained as many punches and kicks on him as I could. He tried to cover his head with his arms but it was no use, I booted him all over the road like a case-ball.

I was hitting so many people, it was like playing Bat the Rat at the amusement arcade. Halfway through the off, two railway police came running out of the station, which was next to us, shouting for assistance. They ran about like headless chickens and clearly didn't know what to do next. One of them was shouting, "Come on, lads, stop." That tickled me. I mean, picture the scene, up to 400 lads half killing each other, and he's shouting, "Please stop. Okay lads, everyone back inside the pub." Don't think so, do you?

We backed the Everton mob under the bridge. Some of them at the front were still trying to be game, but most of them were now backing off. I was in a different zone by this time; adrenalin took over, or was it the coke? I wasn't sure but I was buzzing no end. I heard sirens screaming everywhere now, and it was only a matter of minutes before the inevitable swarm of police came. We quickly attacked again and lads were laid out in the middle of the road, getting kicked all over. The police came in massive numbers and ran about with their batons out, trying to calm things down. When order was restored they put a massive police line between us and the Everton lads. A short while later I walked straight over to their mob near the ground and screamed abuse at them. It was pointless really, but it made me feel better at the time.

We'd got revenge that day, and boy did it taste sweet. They came to us that day wanting it, but I don't think they expected the reception they got. They thought they'd surprise us but we were ready for them and turned the tables. Victory was ours that day, but respect where respect is due, and Everton have my respect all day long.

I returned to town before the match started and took stock over a drink with some of the lads. Everyone was happy how things had gone, except that one of our lads had been slashed across the chest and later needed thirty stitches. We still talk about this day and most agree it was one of the best offs we've had. What made it better is that we were left to it and the police didn't turn up until it was nearly over.

Talking to one of our Intelligence officers at a match later, he told me they'd just sat down to eat in the police station when they got the call, and it took them ten minutes to get there. So, unluckily for them but luckily for us, we got our late Xmas present.

As it takes two to tango, I asked Andy Nicholls, who was there at some of our most violent encounters, to contribute his recollections of the Boro-Everton clashes, from a Merseyside perspective. This is his take on our rivalry.

The phone rang in my office and I picked it up, hoping it wasn't the landlord after his rent again.

"Okay Andy, Paul Debrick here. I'm the big cunt who walked into

your mob at Boro that Boxing Day you got twatted all over, and called you all wankers"

"Pleased to meet you too Paul. I remember you well, very fucking well indeed." At the same time thinking, please tell me your not the big cunt I hit over the head with a fence pole on Scotty Road when we done you the same season.

So this was the "big fella called Paul" my publisher had said was interested in having a chat with me. Apparently he was writing a book and wanted to talk; nothing serious, just after a few pointers and maybe we could be of help to each other. Being a person who rarely gives a fuck, I happily told the publisher to pass on my phone number and I'd see what this "big fella called Paul" had to say for himself. A day later I was sat in my office when he rang, and from the other end came a voice I had never heard, but immediately felt at ease with, as though I had known him for years

The Brick had landed, contact had been made and we chatted for ages, laughing and joking about things we would previously have wanted to injure each other about. That's what it is like today, people who say any different are talking bollocks, footy violence is over, dead, not quite buried but dead all the same. The stuff we spoke about, basically twenty years of toe-to-toes, twenty years of proper hurt, twenty years of slashings, kickings, nickings and dickings, with the odd tactical retreat thrown in for good measure, will never see the light of day in this country again.

In a nutshell, Paul told me about his hooligan memoirs and said that he was not a lover of the genre – "most are a pile of shit" were his words. But of course he soon won me over with his comments that my autobiography, Scally, was the best he had read, not because it's a work of art or well written but "because it tells it as it was, with loads of fucking violence." He went on to tell me he was after other firm's views on Boro's mob and was it okay to use some stuff out of Scally about the clashes we had. I appreciated him asking, as it's very easy to simply rob the odd quote from other books and use it anyway. I'm a fucking master at it!

I told him I would be in touch, we said our goodbyes and when I put the phone down thought to myself, what the fuck was that all about? Having listened to him for twenty minutes I knew I was dealing with "proper Boro" and thought, do I need this hassle, I'll probably upset someone up there and have to face the music. The thing is, I can't cover up cracks or skip issues; if I saw it, I tell it how it was. I'm probably the only hooligan author banned for life from their club for writing a book (I am sure there will another soon though, nailed the same way I was).

I did not have to think long. I was never going to say no, but if the following bit upsets any of you, well yes I am sorry, probably for mentioning the amount of times your lads were cut by ours, but that's the way it was at Everton, we were famous or infamous for it and I won't bullshit you, when our firm was 500-strong, half, maybe more, were knifemen. Boro were not the only firm to get shived, stabbed or slashed, but the difference is, they came back, again and again and again – and that's why we rate them.

The first time I went to Ayresome Park was late Seventies for an FA Cup tie. I was only fourteen, I kept my gob shut and was glad to get home in one piece. The place frightened me. I don't remember much about the day, we lost 3-2 and a Boro lad was stabbed up the arse, meaning the coaches were held back by the police while they looked for lads with blood on them There were plenty, by the way, as their lads had given as good as they got, they always did and it never changed in the twenty-five years we played each other while I was bang at it.

I'll be honest and admit none of our lads even knew Boro had a firm until they turned up years later for another FA Cup tie at Goodison. I was one of ... well, it wasn't fucking many that were in the Crown pub near Lime Street Station when they bowled in and the lad leading the mob ordered 160 pints of bitter! I looked at the doors and coming through was a tidy firm; it was more than tidy it was awesome, and I knew that if we did not get out, we were fucked. The few Everton lads dotted about in there all thought the same and there were a few half empty bottles of Skol left on tables as we did a vanishing trick Paul Daniels would have been proud of.

We didn't go far, just the next pub, The Yankee, and soon returned with a mob I knew was not big enough, but a mob that would at least let them know they were not at Norwich and the day would not be plain sailing. The fight was brief and violent and yes, we came off second best. One lad was thrown through Patches window. I always thought he was Boro but am now led to believe he was one of ours. Today that fight in the middle of the street would mean at least thirty doors needing new hinges the following week, and people would get jail, no doubt. Then it got you a smack with those long sticks from the evil coppers and a warning if you did not fuck off you would get one shoved up your arse.

At the ground we told the lads that Boro were about. A few laughed, a few doubted, but not for long. It was one of the best days at Everton, running battles in the streets, fighting in the ground and a replay at their place to look forward to. I will always remember the Boro end chanting "Figaro" or something all game. I never knew why.

After the game it was a free-for-all. Boro were one of the few mobs, you could count them on one hand in those days, who came out of the Park End and went for it. It was even, a couple were slashed and that was it until the replay or so we thought. An hour later, the window came through in the Red Brick, an Everton stronghold, and that is when the rivalry really started. Any firm prepared to come down there and do that was game, very fucking game. Another lad was cut and the police soon ended what could have been a vicious brawl. Boro, you were lucky that night, the whole of County Road was gunning for you.

You may not believe this but we turned up at the replay. Another Middlesbrough author says we didn't, I'll tell you we did. We were boxed off by the police and had an armoury of weapons with us; we

THE BRICK

knew we needed them. How we laughed when Trevor Steven scored in injury time of extra time and we laughed louder when we won the toss for the right for home advantage in the second replay. We got back to the buses in one piece, unlike many who were in cars and vans. It was a bit daft Boro battering them when they had to come back down in a week, wounds not healed and all that.

The second replay was carnage. Again they brought it to Everton but this time many who were picked off at Boro days earlier were after revenge and tooled up. The end result was that a dozen or so were chopped up, with one poor lad losing an eye according to the papers, who revelled in it all. It was all mindless and senseless, but at the time a part of football violence in the mid-Eighties.

After that night, for years they came to us, we went to them, casualties on both sides, wins and losses, bad days and good days, but apart from the very odd occasion we always had it with each other and each gained the respect of the other.

One of my best days out was one shitty end of season game at Ayresome when we fought all the way from the station to the turnstiles at the ground. No-one took a backward step all day, not one step. The other was at The Riverside, when we went on minibuses to Darlo and arrived in Boro's boozer unannounced. Shut the fire door behind you on the way out, lads!

Frank Sinatra sang, "Regrets, I've had a few, but then again too few too mention." I have had more than a few at Boro, believe me and I take no pleasure in mentioning them. One was walking around Ayresome thinking I was blending into the crowd, trying to bunk in the seats, getting sussed and being surrounded by a moody firm of Boro Yoof! I had a pair of sheepskin mittens on and the lads were ripping me. I plucked up the courage and mocked, "You'll all be wearing them in about a year." The reply came with a smack in the mouth, the taxing of the said items, and the warning to "fuck off now before I take your bubble coat."

Another was getting nicked at The Riverside and turning up in court a day late. Bad move. This was the same court that was full of lads with their names tattooed on the back of their necks.

The worst was the Boxing Day sketch. I won't go into detail: read *Scally*, read *The Brick*, two books, same story, bar a few minor discrepancies. Officially voted the worst day of my life off the pitch, and a lesson learned that Boro don't get mad, they get even. Still I still think we did okay for the first couple of minutes, until their extra 300 turned up!

After that it died a death and things calmed down between us, maybe we all got too old. I was the one who walked into Sam Dodd's and drank with you all before one game. Hutch watched my back and we all agreed it was still on if we wanted it, with the request, "Tell your lads, no steel." It never happened and is not such a bad thing, as at least no-one is in jail, and we are all here to tell our own tales.

At the end of the day, Everton were as good as most firms on their day, when football hooliganism was at its height. Only bell-ends who act hard on their dad's PCs will argue the toss. During this time Boro were regarded as our bitterest rivals. That is not an insult, it's a compliment. They earned the respect of our main lads, and very few firms did that.

Their firm was hard and, in the main, although Barnsley will disagree, fought fair. Like I said I won't bullshit, Barnsley slate Boro for what happened that day. I interviewed them for a new book about the history of every firm in the country (entitled *Hooligans – what else?*) and to this day they call Boro and call them big time for it. Knowing Paul as I now do, I am sure it will be an episode he includes in this book, as he, like me, tells it as it is. And if some people don't like hearing it as it was, I am also sure he will, in his assured manner, tell them to:

"Fuck off and read about Harry Potter instead!"

DERBY COUNTY

I'VE BEEN TO Derby countless times, from the old Baseball Ground with the tin sheets down the alleyways to the new Pride Park stadium which, incidentally, is very similar to the Riverside in Middlesbrough. We used to take a massive mob down there. Just after Euro '96 we took quite a large mob down by train and arrived in Derby around 11 am. We left the station and came out on to the road where we had been told that their main boozer was and headed straight for it. A couple of Derby's lads spotted us and they were surprised at how many we'd brought and mentioned that they'd seen us in London at the England-Scotland game.

We entered the pub, which had just opened, so obviously none of their lads had arrived. The two Derby lads stayed outside and got on their mobiles, telling their lads we were mob-handed. We all got drinks and soon enough we were taking calls off some of their lads asking about numbers. We told them, "Come to us, you know we're here." How I have always seen it, you get into someone's city all up for it and mob-handed and you get their early, you've done your bit, and their mob should come and make a show, but it wasn't always like that. Most of the time they'd get in touch with us and tell us to go looking for them. I've lost count how many times mobs have come to Boro and, within minutes,

111

we'd be there fronting them. That's what it's all about. If you just want to sit there and drink and have a few lines, what's the point, it's a wasted journey. You can sit at home and drink and talk a good off. You don't get it unless you're prepared to look for it and most of our lads were prepared to look, that's what made us a good mob right through the years. We've got our share of idiots that think wearing a Stone Island coat makes them a football hooligan but the majority of our lads are good, sound, game lads who love an off.

The police arrived outside the pub in large numbers, making it difficult for the Derby lads to come round and have it with us. One of my mates from Acklam had known some of the Derby lads for a while and had been on the phone to them. He told me that they were in a boozer just a short walk towards the city centre and asked if I wanted to go and meet them. "Yeah, nice one," I said, so we both finished our drinks and set off to their pub. I thought the police would stop us but when I told the coppers outside the pub door we had to go to the mini bank, he let us go.

We arrived at their boozer and walked straight in to a large mob of Derby's lads and started talking. One large black lad seemed to be in charge of them and he must have been their top boy. I was introduced to him and he told me he was pissed off that we'd got there so early and there was fuck all they could do about it because of the large police presence, but we agreed to do our best to get together.

We left the pub and immediately outside were members of the Football Intelligence Unit. Fuck me, I thought, they've sussed me right out.

"What are you doing in there, Debrick?"

"Having a drink," I said and walked straight past them.

One of them shouted, "If it goes off today you're nicked for organising it."

"Yeah, yeah."

I made my way back to our lads. As I walked towards the police outside where Boro were drinking, one big copper at the front was giving it the big 'un, staring at me with that I'm-hard-as-fuck stare. You always get these coppers who, when they find out you're a top lad, just want to stare at you as if to say, "Step out of line and you've got me to deal with." Meet the same ones in town on a Saturday night when they're out for a drink, or bump into them when they're doing their weekly shopping in Netto, and they wouldn't even make eye contact. Never mind lads, if it makes you feel important then stare away.

We went back into the pub, had a few drinks and talked about what the Derby lad had said. There was not much chance of an off with so many police outside. When it was getting on a bit we decided to make our move. We all left the pub together and, to our surprise, the Old Bill let us walk towards the centre and didn't try to put us in an escort. We made our way round to their pub and some of their lads came running out. It went off briefly in the middle of the street but the Bill were quickly on top and sent us back down the road.

We went down the road and then doubled back and went back towards their pub. Their mob came from around the corner with the big black lad at the front swinging wildly with what looked like a large bunch of keys. We steamed them on a grassed area but the Old Bill was quick to move in on us, and a couple of lads, including the lad with the keys, got nicked. He had been swinging the keys about like a loon right under the watchful gaze of the police, a sure-fire way to get nicked. The police weren't taking any chances now and they hemmed us in and formed a tight escort round us and took us up to the ground.

We watched the game, which was shite, and when it had finished we regrouped, left the stadium and walked down a long main road that led back into the city centre. We somehow slipped the police, although our two spotters were tailing us. A huge black lad blocked our path. He was standing on his own in the middle of the road shouting, "Come on then." I thought, this cunt's either very hard or very fucking stupid. There were 100 of us mobbed up and he's in the middle of the road, facing us, shouting at us to come on. Come on! We quickened the pace and I thought, you're gonna get it, mate. I ran straight at him and he was squaring up to me when one of our top lads drop-kicked him in the chest and sent him staggering backwards, nearly putting him under a bus. He regained his composure only to be kicked by the same lad again and he was away on his toes. Wise decision, I thought.

Derby's firm were a few hundred yards up the road so we all trotted towards them thinking we were going to have it with them properly, when from nowhere came the police, totally mob handed. They always seem to spoil things, don't they? We were so close but so far away, it was a disappointing anti-climax to the day.

NOTTINGHAM FOREST

WE'VE HAD A lot of history with Forest over the years and I rate their mob as good as any in the country. One encounter was at the old Ayresome Park ground. They'd brought quite a large firm up to Teesside, but what happened after the game was something nobody expected. As their mob was being escorted back to their coaches, a small but tasty section of them broke away and attacked the Middlesbrough lads waiting to ambush them down one of the side streets. A fight took place and, even though some of the Forest lads had got done, one whacked a Boro lad over the head with a crate of some sort and killed him. This created a manhunt and, eventually, the attacker was brought to court and jailed. This really pissed off the Middlesbrough lads and from then on Forest were one of our arch-rivals.

On another occasion, 100 of them visited the Riverside Stadium, having travelled up by train, but as soon as they were into Middlesbrough they were swarmed over by the police. It's a usual scene now when you visit Middlesbrough, the police seem to have it well sussed. They were escorted up to the Riverside with us well in tow, and it was the usual banter between the two mobs but not a chance of an off. We went into town for a drink while the match was on and people were commenting on what a sound mob they had. We returned to the Riverside just before the final whistle to see what was going on, but Plod had it sussed again. They were escorted back to the station and for a brief moment it nearly went off, but the police charged us with horses and dogs and sent us scattering.

I went home at this point to get ready to come back into town to work the door that night and, as I left, around thirty of our lads jumped into taxis and a minibus and shot through to Thornaby train station. It's a tiny station, around two or three miles from Middlesbrough, and because Forest's lads were on the train, our lads knew it would be stopping at Thornaby, so they were going to get there before the train and ambush them. The plan worked a treat; they arrived at Thornaby and there wasn't a copper in sight.

There was only a handful of police on the train, so a free-for-all was about to erupt. As the train stopped, the Boro mob attacked, and pulled open the doors. Forest's lads panicked at first, totally shocked at our ambush. The lads nearest the doors got whacked all over. Fair play to our lads, there were only about thirty of them and more than 100 Forest.

It wasn't long before the tables were turned. Forest jumped out of the doors further down the train and mobbed up on the platform. They ran forward and attacked. Give our lads their due, they stood and fought but, in the end got totally done. A couple of my mates who were there said Boro lads were knocked out here, there and everywhere, and were kicked to fuck. One particular mate said, "All I could remember was opening the train door and then next thing I was waking up in the recovery position on the platform."

Forest chased the remaining lads up the platform, and then the police arrived in massive numbers and started nicking people. They weren't amused at all. They had thought the Forest mob were safely on the train and on their way home. What they hadn't counted on was how cunning we could be when we were in search of an off. Every game after that there was a heavy police presence, both at Middlesbrough and Thornaby, just in case we did it again.

Towards the end of the Nineties we made the trip south to Nottingham with a massive mob. We met up in the Cricketers Arms pub, not far from their ground. Our plan worked a treat and by twelve o'clock the pub was packed to the rafters with one of the most impressive Boro mobs I'd seen for ages. We phoned their lads to come and get it but the landlord must have called the police, because, disappointingly, they turned up in force, and had the pub well sussed. There was no way we could get out, due to the heavy police presence, so we decided to sit tight. An hour before kick-off the police decided to escort everyone to the ground, but we had different ideas and fifteen of us left by the back door. They gathered everyone else outside the pub and had them in a tight escort.

A large mob of Forest followed the escort but, unbeknown to them, we were following them. I was at the front with Oathead and the rest were all good lads. We hung back while the police escorted our mob across a T-junction near the ground. Forest's mob was in the street but couldn't get near ours due to the heavy police presence. As we strolled up the road behind them I said to Oathead, "We've got a few seconds and then it's on top." He agreed, so we quickened the pace straight at them. A few of their lads who noticed us coming tried to get everyone's attention, shouting, "Here they are." Too late.

I hit one and Oathead who was by my side clocked another. This was just enough to surprise their mob, and they scattered across the road. I chased two or three of them and trapped them in a shop doorway. Now's my chance, I thought, and was just going to get stuck in when a giant of a copper walloped me across the back with a baton. I spotted another copper running full pelt across the road with his baton above his head and I could tell by his eye contact that his baton had my name on it. Surely he wasn't going to take a run up and whack me with it? Yes he was. I took a massive whack right across the left thigh which felt like it had snapped in two. He raised it again but I didn't wait around to be his target practice.

We were pushed into the Boro escort and I limped to the ground. It doesn't matter how many times you get whacked with those batons, it hurts just the same, even if you're full of marching powder. Right through the game the police spotters were pointing me out and I was convinced I was going to get lifted, but it didn't happen. After the game we all dispersed and three carloads of us hung back and had a drive round to see what we could do, but their lads must have gone for a drink somewhere, so we fucked off home.

Another time, I was working on the door on a Saturday before we played Forest. It was relatively quiet when around sixty Forest came round the corner and walked straight up to the pub. "Where's your lads?" one of them asked me. I was gobsmacked. Normally our lads would have been in the pub where I worked, but it was early, so they weren't. I explained this to them and told them that if they holed up somewhere they would get what they wanted. Too late, the plod must have been tipped off because they appeared and held them all against the wall. I shouted to one of the coppers that they could come into the pub where I was working for a quiet drink, and they'd be okay because we had doormen on. The copper looked at me like I was backward.

"Fuck off, Debrick," he said. "Do you think I'm going to put them in there with you? You'd be straight on the phone to the lads."

He was right first time, but you've got to try, haven't you? Nothing really happened the rest of the day. The police weren't taking any chances after the Thornaby incident but respect to Forest, a good mob on their day, and game too.

Me in a bodybuilding championship in September 2004. Not bad for forty years old, eh?

The old Ayresome Park, surrounded by a rat-run of narrow terraced streets. Many of our lads served their time in those streets.

Two little angels: me (left) and my older brother Mark, aged nine and ten.

Middlesbrough fans in the Seventies: long hair, scarves – and great big boots.

Boro on the pitch in the Eighties and a very different look: the casual era was my time.

The massive Boro section at Shrewsbury in 1986, shortly before it went 'off' in one of the all-time football riots.

The police arrive, only to be scattered back.

Boro lads press into the Old Bill as they pour into our end.

Boro lads, some now armed with lengths of wood, holding the police at bay.

A load of the Boro lads at the Holland v England game in Rotterdam.

Some of the Boro boys leading a charge down the street in Rotterdam.

A Boro mob in London. If your eyesight's good you can see me standing under the lamp-post on the right, wearing a baseball cap.

Some of my Middlesbrough mates gather in the Old Town square before a England v Poland game.

He'd look well in any police line-up: me and my old mate Lee 'Oathead' Owens,

The lads with obligatory tour flag for Italy v England in Bologna in the 1990s.

My good self being cool, early 1990s. By this time I was working the doors in Middlesbrough.

Still two angels: with my brother Mark (right), another big lad, as you can see.

Lads outside a bar in Belgium during the Euro 2002 Championships.

Boro on the march: leaving the hotel in Belgium in 2002.

Cheers Oathead! The big fella and some of the boys enjoying a drink at Euro 2002.

Me and my son Tommy. A chip off the old block, wouldn't you say?

My better half: the lovely Elaine, July 2005

Tommy, Elaine and me at a family wedding at Ford Castle in June 2005.

CARDIFF 1994

THE FOLLOWING CHAPTER is by another of our top lads. He wishes to remain anonymous.

From the minute the FA Cup draw was made and we were paired to play Cardiff City, every lad in Middlesbrough was on a top buzz. Despite the hoolie scene being a bit quiet, we were still taking a decent-sized firm away from home every game and were up for anything. Cardiff were the mob of the moment and a chance to have it with the famous Soul Crew was a mouth-watering thought.

Throughout the Eighties, Cardiff were just an also-ran. Even though they had the numbers they wouldn't have rated in anybody's top ten, but during the previous three or four seasons they had built a reputation for turning out in massive numbers and being game, even going through police lines to get at other mobs. They were even kicking off inside football grounds, so as you can imagine, no one wanted to miss this opportunity to show our Welsh counterparts what we were made of.

A steady stream of lads came back to the games in advance of the Cardiff clash. They wanted to know what the crack was for the Cardiff game and didn't want to miss it. We decided to travel in small numbers to avoid any unwanted police attention, using different modes of transport before mobbing up in Newport to make our assault on the Welsh capital.

The day of the game meant a middle-of-the-night start to get into Wales early and make our presence felt. The coach picked up the Stockton lads in the High Street at 3am and then picked up the rest of the lads in various places. We had around 110 lads going by road and sixty on the train. The coach was the shittiest I have ever seen in my life, a fucking wreck. Coaches don't normally look like that until we're getting off them but this one was wrecked from the start. It was colder on board than it was outside, and with the rain piercing in from the holes in the skylights, everyone spent the whole journey with their coats on. What a nightmare.

In spite of the driver getting lost and the bus breaking down, we made it to Newport in good time and went straight into the pub opposite the station for a couple of drinks and to meet the rest of the lads. When we were all together, we caught the next train to Cardiff. We pulled into the station around noon and marched into the city centre. To our surprise there wasn't one copper in sight. We expected them to be everywhere, especially for a game like this, but they were nowhere to be seen. We marched up the road to a junction, did a right and spotted a pub about 100 yards up on the left. Faces were pressed up against the windows and a few lads came out onto the street, but they took one look at what was coming and quickly ran back in and locked the doors. That was all the encouragement we needed and we set off at a steady jog, straight for the pub. We had only been in Cardiff two minutes and it was about to go off. We were going to smash up the pub and everyone in it.

As we approached the pub a couple of our lads who had travelled by train came running out of another pub opposite, shouting for us to stop. They explained that they had met some Cardiff lads earlier and they had asked for some time to mob up properly. As we didn't want any excuses when it went off, we agreed and joined the rest of our lads in a pub called *The Albert*. This pub was ideal because it was on two levels, with an upstairs room overlooking the main road outside. We also had an excellent view of the pub where Cardiff were mobbing up.

We made ourselves at home and the drinks started to flow. A couple of our lads became restless and wanted to do Cardiff straight away, rather than wait until they had their full mob, but the rest of our lads persuaded them to wait. It was decided that if Cardiff and their Soul Crew hadn't made their move on our pub by 2.30, then we would make our move on them.

Around 2.15 the shout went up that the Soul Crew was here and coming straight at us. The road was full of their boys. Cardiff lad Tony Rivers reckons in his book *Soul Crew* that they only had sixty lads out but he is talking crap. They had their full team.

The first fight we had was with each other as we all tried to get out of the pub. Everyone wanted to be out first, but we were squashed into the main entrance hall of the pub with a single doorman holding the door shut. Bottles and glasses were smashing outside and he must have thought the pub was going to get wrecked. We quickly explained to him that if he didn't get the door open we would smash the pub up from the inside out. At that, he opened the doors and we piled on to the pavement, straight into the waiting Cardiff mob. The whole thing went totally mad. Cardiff were straight on top of us, trapping us into the doorway. People behind me were screaming to get out but it was total chaos. A couple of our lads sprayed CS gas at the Cardiff mob and they backed off briefly, giving us enough time to get everyone outside, and then it went off big time. The whole road came to a standstill; all the traffic stopped and there were dozens of lads walking round half blinded, half choking from the gas. The daft thing is, quite a few of our lads got sprayed as well.

The gas backed Cardiff into the middle of the road and we took the opportunity to steam them. We ran forward and I whacked anybody within punching distance. Everywhere I looked, lads were having running battles and their own little one-to-ones. Give Cardiff their due, they were well up for it, but we wanted it that little bit more. We stood toe-to-toe with them for what seemed like ages and, in the end, split them into two separate mobs. We sent one mob back towards the station and the other up the main road. We followed the larger mob towards the station. We surged forward again but they were on their toes despite having some good lads at the front. The rest were just doing a lot of shouting and didn't really want to know.

A shout came up that the other, smaller Cardiff mob had regrouped and was now on the attack. We turned and steamed straight at them for a full-on assault. They seemed to stop in their tracks and then scattered back up the road. There were a couple more half-hearted attacks by Cardiff, but by now they were only going through the motions in order to save face.

We had come into Cardiff mob-handed, took it to them in their own backyard and got the result we were after. The usual sound of police sirens was everywhere. We stood together, all acting dead innocent. Cardiff's mob seemed to disappear, except for one huge lad who had been out shopping with his wife and decided to launch a one-man attack on our full mob. He must have been off his head or something, but he was game as fuck all the same. Four or five of our lads put him on his arse and when he was down one of our lads raised a glass to do him, but was stopped in his tracks. I know things do happen in the heat of the moment but to glass him would have been totally out of order, even if he was Welsh.

The police finally got us all together and escorted us straight to Ninian Park. They were okay with us, not at all heavy-handed, and I firmly believe they let us do what we did to teach the Cardiff boys a lesson. As we approached the ground we could see hundreds of Cardiff's lads coming from everywhere but, despite making plenty of noise, they just seemed to stand and watch us go by without any real attempt to get at us. (*The Soul Crew* book reckons this is where they did thirty of our lads but the truth is none of us got done that day.)

That was it for trouble. A good day all round, with us doing what we set out to do. A draw meant a replay back at our ground. They kept us back twenty minutes after the final whistle and when we came out there wasn't a soul about. We were escorted back to the train without so much as a bad word from anyone. Apparently, Cardiff had heard that we were parked up in Newport and left the ground early. They caught a train there but the police wouldn't let them off and sent them straight back.

The replay, a week later, was a big disappointment. We had one of the biggest home firms out in years but it was a complete no-show from Cardiff in the town centre. When we got to the ground, we saw that they had brought big numbers for the game but we felt let down that they hadn't made more of an effort to come into the centre and bring it to us.

Whenever we were in the FA Cup draw after that, we looked out for Cardiff as we would have loved to have another crack at them and I am sure they felt the same about us, but the banning orders dished out in big numbers on both sides made a re-match less and less likely. Respect to Cardiff though for being game.

EURO 1996

England were to play Scotland at Wembley during Euro 1996, and the build-up and hype to this game was unbelievable. According to the papers, Scotland would invade the south and there would be riots in the streets. As any English hooligan knows, when you get a chance to play Scotland at Wembley, you don't miss it. Every English soccer thug was going to be there. We knew we'd have to take a massive mob down and show everyone what we were made of. As if anybody didn't already know.

The word on the grapevine, or should I say mobile phone, was that the Jocks would be coming down mob-handed, with firms from the Aberdeen Casuals, Hibs Casuals, and Rangers Casuals, to name but a few, and would be mobbing up in London to show us that they were a force to be reckoned with. This was a brilliant incentive for us. I thought the papers were right and there would be a riot. A good day out was to be had by all and all that, and here was a chance to show our enemy across the border who was the best. As you can imagine, everyone was excited and up for it. I remember travelling down with butterflies in my stomach. I was on a massive high of adrenalin and cocaine and totally up for it.

Our day started very early in Middlesbrough. We hired two small executive coaches, but most of the other lads travelled by train or car. In total, we had around 150 lads, a pretty tasty mob. All the way to London it was the usual scenario of drinking, snorting, and generally enjoying ourselves. Spirits were really high, the anticipation and the thought of not knowing what the day would bring was a killer but, as we neared London, we knew we'd soon find out.

Many of you know the feeling I'm talking about here, when you're approaching a city and you know they've got a tasty firm, there are no police and the next stop is your destination. I used to buzz like fuck off this feeling, it rates as good as any drug and it's a bit cheaper, too. When I finally arrived at my destination, wherever it was, and as I stepped off the train, I would look back at the mob behind me and, nine times out of ten, we had a good one. I used to feel a strange feeling of pride that we were all here for the same reason, and all willing to do what we had to do. London and Euro '96 was no different.

When we arrived in London we met up in Paddington at the Dickens pub, just outside the tube station, and everyone was anticipating a big off with the Jocks. Several lads from up and down the country came into the boozer, asking who we were. When we told them we were Boro, many lads were shocked that we'd brought such a formidable mob down to London. Cardiff's Tony Rivers mentioned in his *Soul Crew* book the moment when we walked out of Paddington tube station and even he was shocked at the size of our mob.

We were told there was a large mob around the corner from our bar so we downed our drinks and went to find them. When we approached the junction near the station a large mob of lads was coming towards us. There were no coppers in sight and two mobs were now going to clash. We wasted no time and went straight across the road, straight at them. I whacked the first one flush on the jaw and he staggered backwards and hit the floor.

Then the mob we were fronting shouted, "We're English, we're English". There was a brief pause, then one of them shouted, "We're Sunderland."

"Wrong answer," I said, and smacked him right in the clock, scattering him back on to the road.

By this time the rest of our mob had come round the corner and the Sunderland lads were in full retreat. A couple of them were unlucky in that they weren't too nimble on their feet, and received a kicking. They eventually all ran up the street and we could hear police sirens screaming away, so we quickly made it back to the bar. Adrenalin was now pumping; we'd had our first taste of what was to come, and we wanted more. Even though they weren't the Jock enemy, they got it anyway. Any mob that we would come across that day was now the enemy, we decided, and were going to get some of the same. Anyone was fair game, whether they were English or Scottish, it didn't really matter, and we didn't give a fuck.

A short while later we were told that Chelsea had a mob out and were drinking a couple of tube stops away from us. There was a mass exodus from the pub again, and it was on to the tube. Not one of us paid on the train, we never used to in London. A hundred or so lads all together, no one pays. It's just a case of hopping the barriers.

When we arrived where the Chelsea mob were supposed to be it was a false alarm, much to our disappointment. There were only around thirty or forty of them and the police quickly sent us back to the pub in Paddington which we'd now established as our base for the day. There were 150 of us but only around thirty actually went to the game, which was typical of us. I've lost count how many times I've been to a different town or city and not been to the game. Like I said earlier, football is shite, it was the other side of it I liked.

THE BRICK

There was a real buzz about the bar as it got nearer to kick-off and we were convinced we'd bump into the Jocks at some point in the day. We decided to make a move, so jumped the tube again and headed for Kings Cross. We were looking for other mobs, but had no luck, so we holed ourselves up into a bar down a side street and decided to watch the match. A short while later someone shouted that Leeds were outside. I flew out of the door and, to my surprise, there was quite a large mob of Leeds lads coming towards the pub. However, there was no chance of a kick-off because riot police had formed a solid line between the two mobs.

The Leeds lads decided to go in a pub opposite ours, but the police stayed with us at all times, right throughout the game. I went into their pub to suss out what was what, and told a couple of the Leeds lads to come and join us for a drink. A handful of them came over, but their main mob refused. It was a good job, because if they had they'd have been immediately ambushed. I think they knew this and that's why they stayed put. They call themselves the White Rose of Yorkshire. It should be the White Handkerchief of Yorkshire.

Everyone used to go on about the Leeds Service Crew but I've never rated Leeds. Every time we've been there, and I've lost count how many that's been, we always went early and we were always up for it but Leeds never really made a show. We would find a pub and be mobbed up and ready but they never ever showed. If somebody's in your city, mobbed up, you go looking for them. Leeds never did. Every time they came to Middlesbrough we advised them to arrive early to avoid detection, and what did they do? They turned up at 2.45 and got dropped off right outside the ground. If you're not up for it, don't do it. Simple.

Back to the England game. We watched it in the bar and spirits were really high. We'd heard the Jocks were heading towards Trafalgar Square, and would be there mob-handed. We left the pub, told the Leeds lads what we had planned, and asked them if they wanted to come with us. The plan was that if the Jocks didn't turn out, then we would have done the Leeds mob, but they declined our offer. Said they had to go to Harrods because there was a sale on, or something like that. Like I said, White Handkerchief of Yorkshire . . .

We got off at the stop before Trafalgar Square and walked mob-handed. Everyone was well oiled, well coked up, and well up for it. As we turned the corner we were charged by riot police in full battle dress, chased by mounted police and threatened with police dogs. They had that many police there we wouldn't have got within half a mile of the place. They chased us down streets, trying to contain us, but we had different ideas. As we came to a boozer a bit further up the road, a mob of Chelsea lads came out and it went off briefly, but with there being so much plod around we decided to make our way back to base to avoid getting nicked. There were several different small mobs in the pub from Huddersfield, Oldham and Villa amongst others, but by this time the whole street was full of plod, so we just stood talking to them.

All in all, it wasn't a bad day out. We had a good crack, and we'd done ourselves proud for turning out in such force. We never did bump into the Jocks, which was a bit disappointing, but you can't have everything.

INTERVIEW
WITH OATHEAD

THE FOLLOWING IS my interview of my old mate Lee "Oathead" Owens. He, like me, was one of the original casuals and we were both fighting side by side up until a couple of years ago. We go back a long way. Oathead was always a good lad to have by your side when it got nasty!

The Brick
Now then, Oathead, I just want to ask you a few questions about your association with football violence. This is probably the only interview that you have done when you have not been cautioned before it commences.

Oathead
Yeah, you're probably right mate!

The Brick
Can you tell me how you first got involved with football violence and how you felt at the time?

Oathead

My first taste of football violence was against our arch-rivals Chelsea. I must have only been around thirteen or fourteen years old. I was in the Holgate end of Ayresome Park, which was where all the old boot boys and skinheads used to go. Around about two o'clock, a large mob of Chelsea lads came into the Holgate end and charged the Boro fans. Fighting broke out all over and I was stood with two older blokes who were protecting their kids. These two blokes got stuck straight into the Chelsea lads and I decided to join in. Like I say, I was only young at the time but I buzzed with excitement as I attacked the Chelsea lads. I was soon put on my arse but bounced back up and tried to do as much as I could. Eventually the police restored order and, after the incident, I thought back over what had happened and realised I loved it. I was immediately hooked on football violence.

Since then we've had many a row with Chelsea's mob. Some good and some bad. I am actually friends with some of Chelsea's main lads now and our rivalry goes back many years. Had Chelsea tried this same stunt a few years later, when we were more organised, then it would have been a different story.

The Brick

I remember you when you were part of the notorious Stockton Wrecking Crew. What was that all about and how did you get the name?

Oathead

The Stockton Wrecking Crew is a name that still haunts me to this day. Whenever I appear in court for whatever offence, the prosecution always bring up this name and use it against me in any way they can. It came about when a small group of us used to go out robbing from one-armed bandits in the early Eighties. We used to lever off the fronts or backs of the machines and take all the money. If you could have seen the state of some of the machines when we had finished you would know why we were called the Wrecking Crew and it just seemed to stick through many years. It was always associated with violence as well.

The Brick

How many times have you been nicked at football?

Oathead

More times than I can remember, probably twenty or so. One that sticks in my mind is when we were playing away to Portsmouth in the early Nineties. I set off from Stockton with another thirteen lads on the Friday afternoon. I had been to Newark near Nottingham on a previous occasion and I knew it was a quiet place with lots of machines for the boys to rob, so we decided that this would be our first stop, to top up our funds and have a few drinks. When we arrived it was heaving, a different story to when I had last been on a quiet afternoon. We asked a local lad where the best pubs were and he directed us to one that I can only describe as a cave. We quickly realised it was full of Nottingham Forest lads, so we went into a back room as they were giving us the once over. We knew it was only a matter of time before it was going to go off, big time.

Soon, more Forest lads gathered outside, as word had quickly spread that we were in town. They beckoned us to come out on to the streets where they thought they would have the advantage. We waited a short while and then decided not to disappoint them. Out we went and straight into them. There were around thirty of them on the street and we were trading punches as fast as we could. Forest lads were getting laid out left, right and centre, and things were looking good. We eventually backed them off but, to our surprise, with Newark being in a square, all the pubs started emptying and we were their target. They came steaming across the square straight at us and for a minute it looked like we were going to get done.

We continued trading punches for a short while and I noticed some market poles on the ground, obviously ready for Saturday's market. I shouted to the rest of the lads to pick them up. They didn't need telling twice. We steamed into them, poles in hand, and the poles were just the right length to get a good swing. I saw one of the Forest lads get twatted with one of the poles and his head was pissing with blood. As quickly as I could, I whacked his mate. Since we were outnumbered about six to one, we were doing really well. Mind you, it helped that we each had a dirty great pole in our hands and were all swinging like fucking lunatics. The next thing we knew the Old Bill turned up with blue lights and sirens.

We dropped the poles and decided to go back into a boozer. As we looked out of the pub window it was if the whole town was out after us. Next, two of the Forest lads walked in with the Old Bill and pointed out me and my mate. We were immediately arrested and thrown into the cells. We were charged with an affray and spent the next few months visiting the Magistrates Court and pleading not guilty. On the day it was dealt with I didn't turn up in court as I was in Sardinia for the World Cup. However, I learned that I had been found not guilty in my absence. Fucking result, or what?

A few of their lads got sore heads that night. They bit off more than they could chew.

The Brick
Do you think football violence has changed over the years since you started going?

INTERVIEW WITH AN OATHEAD

Oathead

The main thing that has changed is the sentences given out. Nowadays, people are getting hammered for having a bit of a row on a Saturday afternoon. Years ago, in the good old days, you could be involved in a full-scale riot and only get a fine. I don't think the violence has stopped, it's just more organised now. It has to be because the police are well on top now, especially with all the spotters they have. In fact they're a fucking nuisance. Bans are also widespread. Banning orders like mine mean we can't go into the town centre, so any Tom, Dick and Harry can now turn up and claim a result. Before the bans no one just turned up in Boro and got away with it.

The Brick

What would you consider as one of your best rows at football?

Oathead

I've lost count how many good rows I have had. One that sticks in my mind is Newcastle away in the Nineties. It was one of the best offs we've had and was a good result, especially because it was the Geordies. We made our way by cars and vans to Heworth in Gateshead and mobbed up there. When we had our act together we caught the Metro to the Monument station. Everyone was game as fuck this time and all good lads.

We came out at the Monument and bounced up the road to where their lads were in two different boozers. We attacked the first and fighting erupted in the doorway. They did the usual glass and bottle throwing but, within minutes, we had them battered and back in the boozer with the doors locked. Nearly all the windows got smashed in and our lads were jumping through and into the boozer with the Geordies cowering inside. One of my best mates, Tony, got a pint tumbler straight in the lughole as he was climbing through; it was funny as fuck. We battered all the Geordies who were in close range and then moved on to the next pub. All our lads were now buzzing and were even more up for what was to come

We marched up to the next pub and they saw us coming and steamed out of the doorway. But we were too good for them. There were about 100 of us in the street. Some of the shithouse Geordies locked the doors behind their mates, leaving them trapped in the street. We steamed them and they tried to defend themselves. Give them credit, they were brave, but we battered fuck out of them. Eventually, the Old Bill turned up and we went to St. James's Park to watch the game.

Afterwards, they got their act together and mobbed up at the Mayfair in the city centre. When we approached them they came at us with everything they could throw at us, but as soon as they ran out of ammo we steamed them through the city centre and battered the ones we caught. It was a good off all round, especially as it was the Geordies.

The Brick
Which mobs do you rate in the country?

Oathead
Everybody knows about Chelsea, West Ham and Millwall, they've always been good. Other mobs I've always rated are Everton, Cardiff, Man U and Spurs. I've had it with all these mobs in the past and have some memories of the offs. But it's not just the big clubs who have reputations for trouble; some of the smaller clubs deserve a mention too. Darlington always had a very tasty mob; the Banktop 200, as they called themselves, were always up for it, especially when they played us. We had some riots when we played them, and I mean riots. They don't

have the mob they used to due to hefty jail sentences and banning orders.

Hull City also deserve a mention. We've got a lot of history with Hull, going right back to the early Eighties when we turned them over in that famous friendly night match. Wigan were game as fuck and they stood toe to toe with us for ages. There is still a lot of violence all over the country, both at big and small clubs. I don't think it will ever stop. I am banned myself but I am still in touch with all the active lads. Good luck lads.

RECIPE FOR DISASTER

RECIPE FOR DISASTER, or dish of the day? Make up your own mind

I've always considered myself as a bit of a chef. In fact, before writing this book I was going to bring out a cookery book, but Jamie Oliver and Gordon Ramsey didn't need any more competition, so I decided against it.

One particular recipe I've used for years, which I love, always left a sweet taste in my mouth. I'll share this recipe with you; some of you will be familiar with it.

INGREDIENTS
(1) A Boro mob, anything from 50 to 400 – doesn't really matter how many, results will be the same.
(2) Inter-city train
(3) Alcohol
(4) Cocaine
(5) Pub
(6) Strange city or town
(7) Home mob
(8) Streets

THE BRICK

METHOD

(1) Take a Boro mob and let them stew overnight.

(2) Take the mob and place them on an inter-city train, the earlier the better, as the results will depend on this.

(3) Add the alcohol to the Boro mob. Doesn't matter which alcohol you use, but don't be shy with it.

(4) Add in the cocaine. Too little or too much can spoil the overall effect, so use the right amount. The Colombian variety is best.

(5) Let the mob simmer for a while until the alcohol and cocaine is well mixed. You should now start to see where this dish is going.

(6) Add more alcohol and a pinch of cocaine every thirty minutes or so according to taste.

(7) Take the Boro mob out of the train and place in a strange town or city. Leave them there for anything between five minutes and a couple of hours, depending on the home mob.

(8) Place Boro mob into pub and allow to simmer, again adding more alcohol and cocaine.

(9) Now add home mob and spread evenly in the streets outside the pub.

(10) Bring both mobs to boiling point and your dish is now nearly ready.

(11) Do not use Leeds mob in this dish as it makes the whole thing a little "runny", if you know what I mean.

(12) Spread the Boro mob amongst the home mob. You must be quick though, because it will soon go "off".

(13) If you follow this recipe to the letter it should leave a sweet taste in your mouth.

(14) Do not add any police to this dish, as it will spoil the overall taste.

WEST BROM

A COUPLE OF years ago we played West Brom at their ground. I hadn't been for a few games but all the lads were going to this one. I was persuaded to go by a couple of our lads and I thought, what the hell, it'll be a day out and we'll have a few laughs.

We got to our coach pick-up point early on the Saturday morning and for a while I didn't think we'd be going anywhere. There'd been a mix up with the bus and it didn't show for a while, but after a few frantic phone calls it turned up.

We boarded the bus and sat on the back seat. Some of the lads in my company at the back hadn't even been home from their Friday night out and were still off their tits. Despite this, the journey was pretty uneventful and we arrived at our destination in Solihull around eleven o'clock. As we pulled up outside the boozer I noticed that the Redcar lads were already there, and there were a few carloads of our lads as well. We had quite a tasty mob.

Birmingham City were at home to Tottenham that day and someone had been on the phone to one of Tottenham's lads, who said they were drinking in PJ's bar in Birmingham city centre. That was to be our next destination and, after a few drinks and some marching powder, we got taxis down to Solihull train station, where we boarded a train to the city centre. We got off one stop early and marched out of the station.

I was up front, and as we came out I noticed five black lads all Aquascutumed up and figured they might have a mob round the corner waiting for us. But when the rest of our lads turned the corner and the black lads saw how many we were, they ran like fuck. We had no police with us as such, just one or two coppers who had clocked us in the station, so I thought as soon as we got to PJ's it would go mental.

We crossed the road and walked a short distance to a road leading up to a T-junction and spotted the bar. Up we went and I said, "Here we go," but Tottenham weren't there. My mate phoned their lad again and he said they were just at the top of the road we were on and to the right. Nice one, I thought, we're gonna get it here. We started to walk the short distance but by now there were quite a few coppers with us and they were asking, "Where are you from?"

"Tottenham," came the reply, so the silly cunts walked with us to Tottenham's pub. One of the coppers must have had a bit more off than the rest of them because he realised where we were from and called in on his radio. As we approached, they blocked off the junction with cars and vans, herded us all against the wall and hemmed us in while a police helicopter hovered above. When we realised how close we were to Tottenham's pub we were gutted, it was only about 100 yards away and we'd nearly got there.

The Old Bill held us for what seemed like ages and then decided to escort us through the city and on to West Brom. Nothing really happened before the game but Oathead was on a coach full of loonies from Stockton and apparently they had a bit of an off and ended up chasing West Brom all over.

After the game we were to meet our coach back in Solihull, as were the Redcar lads, so we came from the ground and got a local train back to Yates's in Solihull. Before we got on the coach we needed some cans and bottles for on the way home and went to an off licence around the corner. As we walked in, you could see the Asian shopkeepers rubbing their hands together as their shop started to fill. They must have thought they were quids in, loads of business and all that. By the time our lads left they had pillaged the shop. People were walking out with just about anything. It was funny to watch; the whole bus was swamped with drink all the way home. There was that much drink that loads of people left bottles of WKD and cans all over the bus when they got off in Middlesbrough. The driver must have been pissed for a week when he collected it all.

All in all, not a bad day out, though it would have been better if we'd got to the Tottenham lads.

KEEPING THE PEACE

I NEVER SET out to be a doorman, never wanted to be one. When I was a young lad the doormen were the enemy, probably because I had loads of run-ins with them. I became a doorman towards the end of 1987. My brother, Mark, was already working the doors at the time but the job never appealed to me.

I used to go into town on a Saturday night with a set of lads who would fight in nearly every pub and every nightclub we went into. I loved this little set-up, because, looking back, I suppose I was a bit of a thug. If there was another group of lads in the same pub, which inevitably there was, we'd make up some lame excuse and start a massive brawl. We'd have an off in nearly every pub we went to. It was mad, really, but at the time I thought it was brilliant.

We went to a well-known nightclub near the Town Hall every week and, if the door lads had any trouble, they would ask us to back them up. On some occasions, if they didn't like a particular group of lads they'd ask us to go and start trouble with them. We were in our element. We were getting in the club for free, and we had the doormen's blessing to fight. It was a pretty strange set-up, I know, but one we thrived on.

The head doorman, whom I knew quite well, asked me to start

working at the club on a Friday and Saturday night. At first I refused his offer, I was happy doing what I was doing. I was enjoying myself, fighting, womanising and drinking. He pointed out that I could still do what I was doing, but I would get paid for it. I took him up on his offer and turned out the following Friday. It was strange at first. One minute I was being a mindless thug, truly a licensee's nightmare, and the next I was getting paid to stop people like myself causing trouble. Talk about the other side of the fence. I became quite good friends with the head doorman, who had been a good amateur boxer and still trained and sparred all the time. He introduced me to the boxing gym, and I started to train and spar on a regular basis. I loved the boxing training, and took to it straight away.

The gym was in the basement of an old building and, to be honest, it was a fleapit. It stank and was dirty, but we trained in it for years. I'd already put a lot of size on with the steroids I was taking and was weight training like it was going out of fashion. Now that I was boxing training all the time I was becoming quite sharp. I trained like this for years and it stood me in good stead.

I worked the club Fridays and Saturdays and we called Fridays "fight night". Every week there was hell on. I used to keep a bucket of salt water by my back door to drop my shirt in when I got home in order to get the blood out. It was rough as fuck in those old days, but we didn't know any different. It's easy working the doors now, people don't kick off like they used to. Most doormen in town are sound lads but some shouldn't be on the doors. They fill themselves with steroids and think they have a God-given right to be a hard case. Sorry lads, you couldn't have lived with us in the old days.

My first real test came on my first New Year's Eve. There had been minor skirmishes throughout the night, though nothing to write home about. At the end of the night a local restaurant owner came in with his entourage. At the time he was considered a bit of a handful, by all accounts a good amateur boxer. I knew who he was, everyone did, but he didn't know me. When we were clearing the club I asked the owner who was staying back, with it being New Year's Eve, and he'd told me no one was staying, everyone out. I went over to ask the restaurant owner and his small group of people to ask them to make their way outside. The restaurant guy's chef, who was sat down, just looked at me, stuck a lighted cigarette in my face, and laughed.

I jumped back in pain and then leapt forward, cracking him right on the jaw. He flew off his chair and landed in a crumpled heap about three feet from where he'd been sitting. I moved forward and was about to perform Michael Flatley's Riverdance on his head when, out of the corner of my eye, I noticed Mr Restaurant steaming at me. Like I said, he had a reputation for being a bit of a lad, so I turned to front him. He landed with a left hook on my temple and for a second I saw a white flash. I quickly returned fire, connecting with a right hand, and then people jumped in to separate us. He was mates with the night-club owner, who was trying to calm him down, and I was told to go into the reception area to try and defuse the situation.

While I was there everything seemed to calm down. Mr Restaurant came walking through and said, "Who the fuck are you?" I could see it was going to go off again. He then said, "I'll bite your fucking nose off." Just as he was finishing his sentence, I sent him flying backwards with a cracking punch. He nearly went over the counter, then I attacked again. It didn't last long though, as everyone split us up again. He was raging. He'd come into the club on this New Year's Eve, and this young doorman had knocked his chef out and was now attacking him. I could see he wanted to teach me a lesson but I wasn't having any of it. The situation was going from bad to worse and they couldn't seem to calm him down. By this time the club was nearly empty, so I was told to get myself home, leaving Mr Restaurant in the club to calm down. I was raging myself. I was only a young lad, and fresh on the doors, but I was no shitbag, and I wasn't prepared to take any shite off anyone.

I went home and was having a drink with my friend Mickey, Ian, the head doormen where I worked, and our various partners when the door went. My lass at the time looked through the blinds, and she said, panicking, "Paul, they're all outside." I immediately jumped up and, sure enough, Mr Restaurant had come to my front door and there were five or six cars outside. I thought, here we fucking go. I quickly picked up two coshes that I kept by the front door and opened it. The street was filled with his entourage, and I knew he wanted to sort out the earlier business.

"Put the coshes down," he said, "and we'll sort this out."

I stood still with coshes in both hands, and didn't give him a reaction. I surveyed the situation and wondered what my best course of action would be. Should I just go berserk with the coshes, or should I wait for them to attack? He repeated, "Put the coshes down, and we'll have a one-on-one. No one will join in." I thought for a second and then, instead of dropping the coshes and keeping my guard up, like a silly cunt I bent down to place them on the floor. It was a mistake I would never make again. Whack, he hit me with a crunching uppercut and I felt my nose shatter. I was stunned for a second or so, just enough time for him to launch a full-scale attack on my head. He was raining lefts and rights down on me as quick as he could, and trying to half kill me. I could see white flashes before my eyes as each punch connected. The blows weren't hurting me, but I couldn't compose myself because they were coming that fast. One of my eyes was nearly closed now and I thought he'd soon stop, but the attack continued.

I could hear all his mates shouting, "Go on, fucking kill him." I wasn't scared or anything like that. I just needed to try to launch a counter, but I was shaky on my legs due to the number of punches I was receiving. He must have got sick of punching me, because he grabbed my head with both hands and sunk his teeth into my nose and gashed it – I still have the scar to this day – then he stood back and right-handed me for good measure.

He stood back and screamed abuse at me. I wasn't listening, I was too dazed. What seemed like a couple of minutes passed, and I started to sort myself out. He was giving it the usual, "Don't ever fuck with me," and all that shite. My face was swollen, I was bleeding, not a pretty sight. I'd just had a good hiding so, as you can imagine, I was pretty down. Down but not out. I regained my composure and said, "Come on then, you fucking arsehole." He looked at me for a second and I could see he wanted more. He must have been thinking, I've just whacked this young fucker all over, and now he wants it again. By this time half the street was out watching. It was New Year's Eve, so everyone was still up.

All his mates were shouting the same shite, "Give him it again, go on," and such like. We squared up to each other and I wanted revenge. He'd made me look like the Elephant Man and there was no way I was going to lay down and take it. Rage filled my head and I wanted to kill him. I attacked with as much venom as I could. I was connecting with some good shots and, to be honest, I think I shocked him. "Fuck you," I said, as I rained blows into him. He responded and counter-punched.

Everyone in the street was shouting and screaming, and one of the neighbours said the police were on the way. The fighting stopped briefly and he told everyone to get in their cars and fuck off. He was left with just one of his mates and he wanted to fight on. I felt more confident now. While all his mates were there I would have been on to a loser. If I'd beaten him in front of them all I would have probably been attacked from all sides.

We squared up again and I was off the mark like a flash. I hit him with a cracking straight right which sent him off his feet and over a small bush in the garden. I could have easily jumped on his head or kicked him while he was down but I let him get back up. We fought like cat and dog for what seemed like an eternity. Both of us were exhausted and looked like we'd gone ten rounds with a JCB. We were both bleeding from just about everywhere, nose, lips, eyes, you name it. Both my eyes were nearly shut, as were his. We both knew we weren't getting anywhere and, in the end, just looked at each other and laughed. It was strange, I know, we'd just rearranged each other's faces, and now we were laughing at each other.

He told me I was a "game fucker" and held his hand out for me to shake. I refused. The girlfriend I was with at the time was crying and said, "Paul, please shake his hand." She was obviously frightened. I still refused. He said to me, "If you shake my hand it'll be forgotten about, if you don't it'll continue at a later stage." I was too fucked to fight on but I still refused his hand, and said, "Whatever." He left with his mate and I returned to the house. My nose was bitten and broken, both eyes were nearly shut, I was in a daze and everyone told me to go to hospital.

"No," I said, "I need a drink."

I never did go to hospital and a week later I was good looking again. This was one of the hardest fights I've ever had, and even though he'd battered me senseless at first, there was no way I would have backed down, never have, never will. Respect though, Mr Restaurant, it was a toughy.

Those very early days on the doors were tough and I served my apprenticeship when it wasn't an easy job. Before the rave culture and all the Ecstasy flooded in, people just used to get drunk and wanted to fight. I worked the club for a number of years. One of my mates, Gunner, who sadly passed away a couple of years ago, was only ten stones ringing wet, but game as anybody twice his size. Shortly after the club had been refurbished, the owner organised a re-opening night. We turned up for work as usual and were told to be our best behaviour as his family were all in, so we had to make a good impression; sensible and all that.

At some stage the club was pretty full and I was having a walkabout inside when this lad who I half knew came up to me and said he wanted to do someone in. I told him to show me who he was talking about and we proceeded to look for this lad. What he'd done, I don't know and I didn't ask. The lad who'd come up to me had a bit of a reputation and I told him I'd put the other lad outside so there would be no trouble in front of the club owner's family and he agreed.

We came to a corner of the club and the lad said to me, "Him, there." He was only pointing to my mate, Gunner, who was also working the door that night. "I want to fight him," he said. I didn't even give Gunner the chance to reply to him. I said, "You cheeky fucker, I'll fight you," and cracked him flush on the jaw. He came back at me, swinging wildly and a big space opened up. Other doormen came over but said, "Let them fight one-to-one," so we were left to our own devices. He connected with a couple of punches but I wasn't going anywhere. I landed with a corker and he staggered back and fell on to a table full of drinks, scattering the glasses all over those sitting there. I leapt on top of him and punched his face to a pulp, then sunk my teeth into his nose.

As I was doing this I glanced up and, guess who was sat all around the table covered in drink and broken glass? Yeah, only the boss's family. We'd been told to be on our best behaviour, and here I was laid over their table with a mouth full of nose, and a crumpled lad under me. They were horrified, totally stunned. I'll never forget their faces, they were a picture. I knew I'd blown it and I got off the lad, mumbled, "Sorry," or something, and then walked away. They just stood there in silence.

When I returned to reception all I could do was laugh. The head doorman told me the owner was now talking to his family, apologising and all that, and was pretty pissed off. I was sacked immediately and went home, still thinking it was funny. I received a phone call from the head doorman the next day, and he'd persuaded the owner to take me back on as I was a "good lad" and did a good job. I was reinstated less than twenty-four hours after I'd been sacked. Result or what?

We had some right laughs working this club, although it got pretty rough at times. I remember a particularly funny incident (well, I thought it was funny). We'd been working most of the night and there'd been no trouble to speak of, when all of a sudden it kicked off. We ran through the club to where the trouble was, got it sorted, and put the people who'd been fighting outside. A couple of minutes later I was in reception with one of the other doormen, a lad called Jimmy. Now Jimmy wasn't really known for his tact, a bit hot-headed to say the least. Anyway, this lad walked straight up to him, waving his arms and making loads of mad noises straight in Jimmy's face. This went on for a while. I knew the lad, he was a club regular, but Jimmy obviously didn't because he promptly hooked him and put him straight on his arse.

The lad sat on his arse for a while and Jimmy stood over him, looking at him. I said, "Jimmy, for fuck's sake, he's deaf and dumb." Jimmy promptly turned and asked the receptionist for a pen and paper, and then wrote something on it. When he turned towards the lad, who had now got up, Jimmy held the paper up to his face and it read, "Sorry mate." The deaf and dumb lad read it and began waving his arms and was trying to shout at Jimmy, but all that came out were mad noises. We cracked up laughing while Jimmy stood there, red faced.

DIPLOMACY

WORKING THE DOORS in the early days was just one fight after another. Middlesbrough was a rough place to drink. It wasn't always on the door that we got trouble. If some other doormen were getting grief, then we'd get the shout and give them back up. We didn't mind, it was a bit of excitement for us and relieved the boredom of standing there.

One Saturday afternoon I was working at the Shakespeare pub. We used to work a shift from midday until three o'clock, when it was at its busiest. I only did it when we had a shite away match or if I couldn't be bothered to walk up to Ayresome Park. This Saturday I was working with a lad called Mick, a big, thick-set train driver. He worked the door straight after his train shift and arrived with his steel toe-capped boots still on. Many's the time I've seen him put one up someone's arse for being cheeky. They never came back.

I'd known Mick for years and he'd worked the doors for years, well before I started, so he knew the score, and everybody seemed to like him. We'd had a quiet afternoon and we were pretty bored. Both the Shakespeare and another pub called the Masham, about fifty yards away, were on a pedestrianised precinct, so there were no cars around. Around about 2.30, one of the doormen from the

Masham came over and told us there were around twenty-five lads in there who were going to kick off and cause some chew. He said they'd been throwing drinks about and generally working themselves up. They were from out of town, but he didn't know where. We had a word with our landlord and then went to the Masham.

It had an entrance at both ends and you could walk straight through the open-plan bar. We went in the right-hand door and saw, immediately to our right, twenty or so lads fucking about in a corner. The pub was quite busy and I knew most people in there. I could see it was only going to take one daft thing and the whole pub was going go off. The doorman asked me and Mick to stay, have a drink and watch their backs in case anything happened.

"I'll do better than that," I said, "I'll get them out."

I walked over to the group and was about to ask them to calm down when a couple of them stood straight up to confront me. I thought, I'm wasting my time being nice here. I'll try the diplomatic approach. It always seemed to work. I right-handed the first one as hard as I could, and cracked the other right on the chin. And then it went off big time.

All the lads in the corner seemed to jump up at the same time; they all wanted to kill me. "Have I done the right thing?" I asked myself. Too fucking late, the damage was done. Punches were raining down on me from every direction and I backed off a couple of feet. There was a lot of shouting and, as I surveyed the situation, I realised I had a decent back-up with me. Forward I went, throwing punches. Glasses were being thrown and I heard them shatter against the wall behind me. The other doormen and a few local lads were now at it hammer and tongs. The whole corner of the pub was at it; it was like a Wild West brawl. I wish I could have had it on video.

We were getting the upper hand and some of the "out of

towners" were now going out on to the precinct. Only around half a dozen of them stayed and they got a good kicking. One of them was game as a pebble; every time he got put down he was back up, as if he had a spring up his arse. Next thing, from nowhere, a stool came through the air and connected with his head. Goodnight mate. That was the end of him. By now all these lads were on to the precinct, just outside the door, so I picked up a stool and chucked it out at them for good measure.

I turned round and the pub looked like it had been in a bomb blast. Tables were upturned and there was glass everywhere. Someone shouted to me that they were coming back, so I opened the door to see what was happening. The stool I'd thrown out had been promptly smashed up and they were now coming straight at the door with stool legs in their hands as makeshift weapons. The doorway was only narrow, maybe enough to fit two abreast, so I went to go out first. Mick was immediately behind me, followed by the other doorman. When I reached the doorway I was confronted by this big fucker with one of the stool legs in his hand. He had a bloody nose and was screaming at me to come out. I wasn't sure whether or not he'd use the stool leg so I went forward. Big mistake. The stool leg came crashing down straight onto the top of my forehead. I thought he'd break my head like a boiled egg. I was like one of those cartoons characters where they get whacked and a lump appears straight away with birds flying round it. I blacked out and Mick, who was behind me, caught me under the arms and dragged me back into the pub. I must have only been out for a few seconds, because when I came too the lads were still in the doorway shouting for us to come out. They were still armed with the stool legs, so I think anybody else who had the bottle to steam out was going to get what I'd just got.

Next thing, police sirens were going off and Mick half carried me to the other pub door and we made our escape into the shopping centre. To say I was dazed was an understatement. The two brain cells that I did have inside my head were now playing ping-pong with each other and were wondering what the fuck had hit them. I managed to half walk, half stagger, through the shopping centre and Mick said he would take me to hospital. I refused and told him to take me home. By the time we got there my head was splitting and I had a lump the size of a small football on it. I was amazed it wasn't split open. After a couple of hours I got myself sorted and got ready to go to work for my next shift on the door. I got picked up for work and I can't even remember the journey there.

An hour on the door and I had to go home. I kept blacking out and was told I must have delayed concussion. Whatever I had it fucking hurt, but if I was going to get involved in brawls I was sometimes going to come off worse. This time I did, but it was fun all the same. We later found out the lads we were fighting were a group from Sedgfield on a stag night.

BLING

MIDDLESBROUGH IN THE late 1980s was a very violent place to go drinking. It seemed that everybody just wanted to get drunk and fight anyone within punching distance. I've witnessed some horrendous acts of violence over the years. Fortunately, I have a strong stomach.

One particularly vicious incident was when I was working a nightclub door. It was a Saturday night and, as usual, the town was packed with everyone out to get pissed and have a good time. The club I worked had a main entrance that led to a flight of stairs with a reception area at the bottom. Most of the doormen stood at the main door. However, towards the end of the night, the majority moved into the club, leaving just one or two upstairs on the main door. This particular night I was on the top door, as we called it and, surprisingly for a Saturday night in Middlesbrough, nothing untoward had happened. But that was about to change.

Around 1am four very large Rastas walked up to the door. I knew they were out of towners straight away, just by their appearance. They were dripping in gold and all four of them were big fuckers. "Alright mate," they said to me in the broadest Cockney accent you could imagine. "All right lads," I said in broadest Middlesbrough. They walked down to the reception area and I can remember thinking, you don't want to go in there, lads. But who was I to tell them. Not that it had anything to do with them being black or anything, but four big Rastas, dripping in gold, giving it the Cockney wideboy sketch wasn't going to mix with Middlesbrough locals, as they were to find out.

They asked how much it was to get in; it must have only been a couple of quid but they were arguing, saying they shouldn't have to pay. Why, I don't know, because they looked like they were worth a few quid, but they argued all the same. They ended up paying and then disappeared into the club. I thought, it's only a matter of time before we get the call, but a short while passed and nothing seemed to happen. Suddenly, the four came out of the club and proceeded to walk up the stairs towards the exit. Each of them had a can of Red Stripe in his hand and we'd been told no one was allowed to take drink outside. With me being on the top door on my own, it was now my job to stop them leaving the club with their drinks.

When they were halfway up the stairs I said to them, "Sorry lads, you can't leave with your cans. You've got to leave them inside the club." The Rasta at the front looked at me, held his can out and dropped it in front of me, spilling lager all over the floor. The diplomatic approach was now out of the window. I promptly drop-kicked him under the chin, sending him backwards down the stairs into his mates. You cheeky cunt, I thought, don't come in here giving it the big 'un. He fell backwards and his mates tried to catch him, but he was too heavy and they all buckled under his weight.

As they regained their composure they looked at me with pure hatred in their eyes. I thought, here we go. Then the door leading into the main club opened and what seemed like every man in there came steaming out. It seems while they had been inside they had been arguing with some of the local lads and now the Rastas' worst nightmare was about to come true. They tried to fight at first and seemed "game on", but they were quickly engulfed in kicks and punches coming from every direction. They fell to the floor and were booted all over. I could see some of the local lads rip gold chains off their necks and there was not a thing they could do. All four of them received a severe beating, and every bit of gold was taken from them. When they finally picked themselves up, their dreadlocks stayed on the floor. They had been ripped out of their heads. They were in a sorry state. They crawled out of the club and off they went.

Shortly afterwards, some of the locals were waiting outside on the pavement area near a T-junction. A brand new Rover pulled up at the red light and stopped. The Rastas were in it. What happened next was out of order in my eyes but I'm not really one to comment. The car was systematically attacked from all sides, every panel and every window was smashed in and, to be honest, when the attack finished it looked like a scrap car. It was wrecked. They eventually drove off and were giving it, "You're gonna get shot next week," and all that carry on. I wish I had a pound for every time I was going to get shot, I'd be a millionaire. But at the time, with four Cockney wideboys being half killed and robbed, we had to take the threat seriously.

As you can imagine, the next weekend the club was full of every lunatic from Middlesbrough you could think of. Everyone was tooled up, as were the doormen. We could have started World War Three with the armoury we had, but it was for nothing. They never did show up again and I bet they never recommended Middlesbrough for a night out to their mates.

In those days, out of towners weren't welcome. Everyone knew each other on a personal level back then, and everyone stuck together. Nowadays, people are out for themselves and wouldn't think twice of turning their back on you. How times have changed.

THE BRICK

Student Night was on a Thursday and on those nights you could turn left or right out of reception into two separate areas of the club, one for students, one for regulars. Down the stairs came a lad I recognised as a "hard case" from my old school. He was a couple of years older than me and a big lad, so when he tried to get into the student section I asked him to show his Union card. He looked at me as if I had something missing and said, "I'm a student." I knew he wasn't so I said again, "Unless you've got your card you'll have to go in the normal section of the club." He stood and argued the fact for a while and then, as he was leaving, he said to me, "I'll be back to sort you out." Yeah, yeah, I thought. Heard it all before. The night went without any more incidents and I thought no more about it.

The following Thursday came and I was on duty again and who walks in, the same lad, this time with his older brother, whom I also recognised. He came down the stairs and straight up to me, and said, "Which side do you want me to go in tonight, you daft cunt?" I thought, don't beat about the bush, mate, say what you mean.

He then said, "Do you want to go outside with me?"

"Not really," I said, "It's a bit cold."

He looked at me, puzzled and then in a second I cracked him, splitting his eyebrow wide open. He stood stunned for a second with blood dripping from his eye and down his cheek. He looked at me through his good eye and said something, which at the time I thought was funny: "That was a lucky punch. You won't hit me again." How wrong he was. I punched his lights out before he had time to compose himself and he ended up on his arse on the carpet. He picked himself up, looking a bit worse for wear and promptly left the club with his brother in tow. On his way out of the door he was muttering, "I'll be back," and all that shite. I thought, you said that last week, mate.

The manager at the time was an ex-copper who had been quite high up and he saw the incident happen. He told me to go inside and stay out of the way in case the lad came back. After all, he was in a bit of a mess when he left. I went into the club and was talking to a couple of lads when I got a shout to go to reception. When I arrived, three coppers were stood there asking for me. "Paul Debrick," they said, "you have the right to remain silent." They arrested me pronto. The shitbag who had come to the club wanting to fight me had been to the police station and pressed charges. If the shoe had been on the other foot and I'd have come off worse, there's no way I would have done this shithouse trick. You just don't do it, but he was obviously pissed off at what I'd done to him, and he must have thought he'd get me back by having me nicked.

Once at the station, it was the usual scenario. I was searched, my details were taken, then I was placed into a cell and I gathered my thoughts. The lad I'd whacked knew my name and was now in hospital being stitched up. I was bang to rights and I was thinking about what to say when I was interviewed. I was never going to hold my hands up to it, but I knew the police would have taken statements from people at the club. He had a witness too, his brother, who would have been glad to give a statement, so I was looking at a court case. I was annoyed, to say the least, at what he had done, but I was now more concerned at my own predicament.

When you're in the local cells, time seems to drag, and it seemed like I'd been there ages when I heard a key in the door. It opened and I couldn't believe who was standing there on his own. It was the ex-copper who was our manager and he said, "Get your shoes on, Paul, I'll drop you off at home." I took stock of the situation and said, "What, no charges?" He said, "No. Come on then, let's go." I couldn't believe my luck. I mean, one minute I was looking at possible jail, the next, I was getting a lift home with no charges to face.

Happy wasn't in it. I could have kissed the manager but he wasn't that good looking, so I decided against it. I returned to work the next night and heard no more about it. I never did see the lad again. I wish I had, because I would have told him he'd wasted his time going to the cop shop and that he was a shithouse.

BOXING CLEVER

I WENT TO work in another nightclub in Middlesbrough called Madison, now closed down. It was the most popular club in its day, massive, with two separate clubs in one and always packed. I already knew the lads on the door, so I fitted in straight away and we all got on really well. With the club being so big there was a team of about twelve doormen on every weekend. One Saturday night I found out just how good we were.

The North East boxer Glenn McCrory was fighting against a Kenyan called Patrick Lumumba at a well-known local venue for the IBF World Cruiserweight Title. There had been no trouble, but then we got the call to go downstairs. The head doorman informed us that Lumumba and his entourage of American sparring partners and others were at the bar and were being a bit chewy. There were around ten of them, all big, black blokes in suits and some wearing big cowboy hats. They were being quite loud, as Americans do.

As soon as the fight finished they had come into the club and got in free so they should have had a bit more respect, but things started to get a bit boisterous. They were giving it the 'big un', drinking Champagne and shouting their mouths off. They'd got three bottles of Champagne, were refusing to pay, and had said to the head doorman, "What ya going to do about it?" He, in turn, asked me and my brother Mark what would be the best plan of action. I told him we should put them out of the club. "They're not coming in here and taking the piss," I said. He agreed and I could see he was raging at the treatment he'd received from them. They obviously thought they were untouchable. How wrong they were.

We approached them and, as we got near, they all put their glasses down and squared up to us. It's not every week you get a full American boxing entourage in the club, all big fuckers and one of them has just fought for a title (McCrory beat him on points, by the way). I thought, shit or bust here, we're gonna get a kicking. But there's no way I'd have backed down. The old diplomatic approach came into play. I quickly cracked the first one as hard as I could and caught another with a flying head butt, which sent him falling on to his mates. The other doormen were now by my side and the head doorman had knocked one of them spark out on the floor. A few of the lads drinking in the club joined us and it went off big time. We were at it hammer and tongs and, to be perfectly honest, they put up a shitty performance.

I expected a good show but only a couple of them were really game. For a second it calmed down and they just stood there giving it the big 'un, shouting and screaming at us. They called us English scum and so on, and were proper pissed off that we'd had the bottle to say something to them. Then, just as I thought it had calmed down, the head doorman right-handed one of them with what I can only describe as a corker of a punch. He was knocked out before he even hit the floor. His eyes rolled and I could see he wasn't getting up. This sent the situation spiralling out of control and we attacked again. Some of them were laid out on the floor, knocked out, and what made it funny at the time was that they still had their cowboy hats on. We dragged them out and threw them down some concrete stairs into a back alley and they landed in crumpled heaps on top of each other.

When it had calmed down I decided to make a sharp exit with my brother and we fucked off to a club where we'd worked previously. I knew the police would be along and I knew I would get pointed out, so we decided to go to the other club until things blew over. While we were talking to the other doormen we saw police cars with their lights on heading towards our club. Unbeknown to us, the first pair who had been flung down the exit stairs had run out into the street and flagged down a cop car, saying we were killing their mates. They were right, but no need to grass us up lads, eh?

After about half an hour, when we thought things had calmed down, we decided to go back to our club and entered by the bottom stairs. I couldn't believe what greeted us in reception. Five policemen were standing with three of the Americans, who now looked like they'd been ten rounds with Mike Tyson, never mind Glenn McCrory. I said to our kid, "Just walk into the main car park and we'll fuck off." He nodded and we went up the short flight of stairs, out of the door and into the car park.

One of the Americans shouted, "It's them, it's them." We must have taken only ten or so paces when the doors to the club opened again and two policemen said, "Just a minute, lads. Can we have a word?" "Like fuck," I said, and off we ran through the car park with the two of them in hot pursuit. They were shouting, "Stop," as they were chasing us. That always makes me laugh. When coppers are chasing someone they always shout, "Stop." Let's face it, you're not going to, are you? We didn't, and we ran through the car park and then on to the ramp that leads back into the main centre.

The cops were about forty feet behind us and I thought that once we hit the main street we were fucked because it was Saturday night and other police on duty would see what was happening. We left the ramp and turned the corner and, as luck would have it, a taxi had just dropped someone off and was about to pull away. We leapt in and shouted to the cabbie, "Fucking drive." He pulled away just as the two coppers chasing us came round the corner. They looked at the taxi and saw me and our kid on the back seat but it was too late for them. We waved at them through the back window and laughed in their faces. They were sick as fuck. Some you win, some you lose.

The next day we got a call from the head doorman who told us some of our lads had been nicked and the police were after us. Monday came and the local papers were full of the story about how we'd attacked them for no reason. What a load of shite, I thought. They deserved it, cheeky cunts.

As luck would have it, the work permit that Patrick Lumumba had to come over here to box did not allow him to enter town centre licensed premises, for some reason or other, so in the end they couldn't press any charges against anybody. We all returned to work the next week and got a bollocking from the manager who said we could have handled it better. I thought we handled it okay, but my okay and his okay were obviously different.

WICKER'S WORLD

A COUPLE OF years after I'd started working the doors, a new pub opened in Middlesbrough called Wicker's World. Ian, who was running the door in the nightclub, asked me if I'd like to be head doorman there and I jumped at the chance.

It was set on two levels, the upper level having a balcony which looked down on to the lower level. At the time it was smart and everybody seemed to take to it straight away. The opening night was a bit of a posh do. The owner was a well off businessman who'd never been in the pub trade before, and the place was to be run by his two sons, who'd also never been in the pub trade. So to be honest, they were green as grass at first. There was a lavish spread upstairs and there were different coloured cigarettes for the guests in little posh glass bowls on every table. When the bowls were empty they were just refilled, so, as you can imagine, me being me, I was smoking pink, green and yellow ciggies for the next three months. They wanted six doormen to work the weekends, three upstairs and three downstairs. Also, they wanted doormen on every night of the week as they had karaoke nights and special promotion nights through the week.

The first time I had trouble was when I was on the main door. I was just talking to one of the owner's sons when a lad came up, being a right gobshite. I told him he couldn't come in and he stood there calling me a daft cunt. I was in a predicament now. We were outside on the pavement with the owner's son next to me, so I wanted to make a good impression. I looked at the owner's son, who by now was looking sheepish, because, like I said, they were quite posh and I don't think he'd been in a situation like this in his life. The lad kept going on like a fucking idiot, giving it, "Who do you think you are?" and all that shite. I thought, fuck it, owner's son or not, and cracked him flush on the jaw, sending him crashing into the wall and on to the floor. He was spark out and looked in a sorry state.

As I turned to look at the owner's son, his eyes were wide as saucers. "I can't believe what you've just done," he said, and I thought I was in for my first bollocking, but instead he came out with, "Why didn't you do it on the camera?" We had CCTV just inside the doorway He went on, "Next time you wallop someone, will you do it on the camera so I can show my old man." I was gobsmacked, but relieved I wasn't getting a roasting. "No problem," I said. "Just make sure you set the video and I'll see what I can do."

Every time we had a bit of trouble after that, he would come out to the door and ask if anyone had whacked someone on camera so he could go upstairs to the office and watch it. It was a strange thing to do but, deep down, he must have liked a bit of an off himself.

Just inside the door, we had a buzzer-light system on the wall. It looked like a tiny set of traffic lights. These were to alert us of any trouble. Behind the bars were little buttons to press if there was some chew. If the buzzer sounded, as we ran into the pub from outside we only had to glance at which light was lit up to know where to go. The top light was obviously the upstairs bar, the bottom light the downstairs bar, and the middle light the DJ box, which was upstairs as well. Sometimes the DJ would shout to us over the mike as well and direct us to the trouble. There was a large staircase in front of the main door just to the right, and over to the left in the corner was an iron spiral staircase Depending on how busy the pub was, it would only take seconds to get to the incident. It was a pretty good little system.

Working the door one particular Saturday night, we heard the buzzer going off about ten o'clock. I was working the bottom door with Gunner and my brother Mark. As we went through the doorway we noticed that it was the top light, so ran straight up the staircase which brought us to the balcony near the ladies' toilets. There were ten lads fighting, so we split them up and a couple of us proceeded to throw the ones who had been in the middle of the fight outside while other doormen stayed to make sure nothing else kicked off.

When we returned upstairs I noticed one of the doormen, a lad called Mick from Redcar, had a head wound which was pissing blood. Two lads had waited until we had gone downstairs to throw the others out and then attacked the doormen with a Budweiser bottle, which they smashed over Mick's head. He was in some pain and had a large gash. Mick still had hold of one of the lads and another doorman had a tight grip on the second.

We could have phoned the police at this point and pressed charges against these two, but what would be the point? Instead, we took them through the exit door by the ladies' toilets and down the outside metal staircase that led down to an enclosed courtyard at the back of the pub. How we saw it at the time was that these two had been caught smashing a bottle over a doorman's head and now we were judge and jury and were going to dish out some appropriate punishment. Mick's white shirt was now going red with his own blood. I saw red myself but not on his shirt. The red I saw was anger. I mean, having a fight with someone is fair do's, but smashing a bottle over someone's head for fuck-all is out of order.

I threw one of the lads against the wall and cracked him as hard as I could. He staggered a bit and then tried to defend himself but to no avail. I was set on doing as much damage as I could. There was no way they were getting away with this one. I could hear the other lad getting a severe beating behind me as well, and he was calling out how sorry he was. "Yeah, bet you are mate, but you soon will be." The lad I was working on was soon unconscious and I left him in a crumpled heap in the courtyard. I turned round and the other lad was also spark out on the floor so we left them and went back inside to clean up Mick. After a few minutes it was apparent he needed stitches, so off he went to hospital.

Only a couple of minutes had passed and we went back down the courtyard steps to see what was happening with the two lads. I was fucking raging and, as we got to the bottom of the stairs, the lad I'd brayed was now back on his feet helping his mate. "You cheeky cunts," I said and promptly right-handed him again, sending him across the yard. I quickly followed in and proceeded to punch his lights out against the wall.

What happened next was quite funny looking back, but at the time it just made me even more annoyed. As I was punching him, the ground gave way under my feet and I dropped down until I was in line with his knees. I'd been standing on a manhole cover, which had given way under my weight because it had a large crack in it. I quickly jumped out of the manhole, more embarrassed than anything, and hoped no one had seen but the other lads on the door were falling about laughing.

By the time we threw the two lads out of the courtyard they were both in a very sorry state. Their shirts were ripped off their backs and they were covered in blood. The thing is though, if they were prepared to smash bottles over people's heads, then eventually they were either going to jail or they were going to end up getting a good kicking; this time they received the latter. Mick had four or five stitches in his head and came back to work straight away.

In the very early Nineties' rave scene, Ecstasy flooded everywhere. People were going on about this new drug, saying how brilliant it was, and it seemed to quieten the town down for a while. It seemed like nobody was going out looking for trouble anymore. Everyone just wanted to dance and be happy.

I went to raves with my then girlfriend and we both loved it, it was mad. One minute I was on the door being dead sensible, well, as sensible as I could be, the next I was in the middle of a rave, full of E and going for it on the dance floor with my girlfriend. We went to the Stockton rave a couple of times and to be honest it was a bit of a dump, so we decided we'd try the Blue Monkey rave in Sunderland and I couldn't believe my eyes when I walked in. Everyone was going mental and the place was packed to the rafters. The Blue Monkey was the most popular rave at the time and I'd get off work early most Saturdays and go there. I loved the place but it only opened until 2am so when we heard of a new rave around the corner that was open all night, we started to go there.

Every lunatic in the North East used to go and I was very surprised there wasn't loads of trouble. I made some good friends there; everyone seemed to be there for the same reason, which was to get off their heads and have a good time.

While going to these raves I met a lad from the South Bank area of Middlesbrough called Greg, who was also well into the scene, and we became good friends. He's helped me out no end when I've been on my arse and he was there for me when I needed him when I was divorced some years ago.

Speaking of divorce, I'd been to the rave one Saturday night with my then girlfriend and had returned to the flat where I lived. She came with me and I must have been off my nut on E's because I asked her to marry me. She said, "Yes", obviously. Well, she would wouldn't she? Who could refuse an offer like that? Later on in the day when I'd come down off the E's and whatever else I'd taken, I thought to myself, why the fuck did I ask her to marry me? But I went along with it and we set a date for a Monday. Just before the wedding I came out of an all-night rave on a Sunday morning like a buckled wheel, and we were getting married the next day, so I knew it was a sham from the start.

She moved into my flat with this daft cat called Kit Kat (bet that name took ages to think up). Anyway, it was my flat and I had it pretty nice but this horrible furry little twat was pissing all over the carpets and just generally getting on my tits. One day when she was at work, I went into the front room and the cat had shit on my new carpet. Me being an animal lover and everything I did what most animal lovers would have done; I strangled the cat. After I'd killed it I thought, oh, fuck, she's gonna be upset when she gets in from work, what the fuck am I going to do? The kiss of life was out of the question because its breath was too fishy so I popped it into a carrier bag and hatched a plan.

I took the lifeless moggy out in the car to the nearest main road and tipped it out by the side of the road. She came home from work and shouted for the cat to come in. Obviously, no cat arrived, so after about an hour she was wondering where it had got to. "I wonder if it's been up near the main road," I said. "Let's go and have a look." We jumped into the car and, lo and behold, there was the cat still by the side of the road. Well, it would be wouldn't it? It wasn't going to get up and fuck off somewhere. I stopped the car and said, "The cat's dead. It must have been run over." That was it, hysterics for an hour or so. In the end I had to get the cat and bury it, proper funeral and all that. She was so upset I had to go to the pet shop and buy her another fucking cat. In the end I proved everyone wrong. People say cats have nine lives; they haven't. I couldn't believe no-one told her what I'd done to the cat because at the time everyone knew about it. After she'd got over the incident we went raving every weekend and for a few years we spent the weekends high as kites and the weekdays wrecked, getting over the previous weekend.

The job at Wicker's World was ticking along nicely and I loved working there. The many good times well outweighed the bad times, but there were bad times. One particular Thursday night we had a really bad incident which has stuck in my mind ever since. It wasn't that busy a night but we still had a few in and got the call to go to the upstairs bar, as there was some trouble. When I got there with another doorman I saw a group of lads running about like headless chickens, obviously worked up about something. I walked up to see what the commotion was about, I realised one of the lads with this group had been glassed in the side of his neck and blood was pumping out and squirting all over the place. I didn't even ask what had happened. I had to act because I knew this lad was in serious shit and if something wasn't done quickly he was fucked. I've seen many stabbings and glassings in my time but this was one of the worst. He was panicking and didn't seem to know what to do. His mates were more bothered about who had done this to him but the lad who had done it was long gone.

I quickly threw him to the floor and shouted to one of the barmaids to throw me a towel or cloth, anything she had and told the other doorman to phone for paramedics. I told the lad to lay still and shut the fuck up and I would sort him out. The blood was coming from his neck like a water pistol and I was getting soaked. I rolled the cloth up into a ball and stuffed it into the wound and put as much pressure on it as I could. If I could stop the blood flow until the paramedics got there then I knew he would be okay. While working at a well-known oil refinery, I had done an advanced First Aider's course, so I knew what I was doing. I held the pressure on for what seemed like an eternity. Meanwhile, a couple of his mates were actually saying to me, "Get off him, leave him alone." Talk about fucking thick. What did they think I was doing, fucking strangling him?

When the paramedics finally arrived I explained about the wound and said, "His artery has been severed." They quickly got big wads of packing out and as I moved the cloth, the blood spurted out immediately. They quickly re-applied the pressure and off he went to hospital. I knew he was in a serious situation and I had done all I could to sort him out.

A couple of weeks later the lad came into the pub and explained that he'd had surgery, quite a few stitches inside the wound and around sixteen stitches outside. It was a pretty gruesome wound. He said I'd saved his life and asked me if he could buy me something to show his appreciation. I thought about saying, "A new Porsche," but that might have been pushing it a bit. In the end I declined his offer and told him I would have done it for anybody, and was just glad that he was okay.

See, people see doormen on the doors and think it's a piece of piss. Well, it is to a certain extent but then it does have its bad moments, some significantly worse than others.

One Saturday in the mid-Nineties I was working the Wicker's World pub door and it was a typically busy night. I was working on the main door with my brother, Mark when we were alerted by the buzzer going off. We ran into the pub and found the trouble was up next to the DJ stand in the far corner. Some lads had been kicking off with each other, like they do, so we quickly stopped what was going on and started to put the lads involved outside.

I was escorting one lad out down the back staircase when he

started struggling. He was shouting his mouth off and trying to break free so I gave him a slap to shut him up. As we reached the bottom of the stairs he broke free. We were now in a corridor which led to an exit door and then out on to the street. He turned to me, still shouting abuse, and I noticed he had a knife in his hand. He was saying the usual shite, "Who the fuck do you think you are?" I wish I had a pound for every time I have been asked that. I thought about wearing a name badge like they do in infant school so people wouldn't have to ask me, but it would have only ended up getting ripped off, so I didn't bother.

The lad waved the knife at me. He must have thought I was going to shit myself. Wrong. I cracked him as quickly as I could and he staggered into the wall. All I wanted to do was get the knife off him before he used it, so I went straight at him. In the struggle I got stuck in the leg with the knife, nothing major, but the cheeky cunt had used it nonetheless. He broke free, kicked the emergency doors open and bolted. The police must have been parked right outside the pub, because he was pulled straight away.

I went into the staff toilet and checked my leg. I had a small knife wound on my thigh that was bleeding. The police came to the toilet with the lad and asked me what happened. I explained about the trouble and told them someone had used a knife on me and that I now had the knife in my possession. I could see the lad's face and he was shitting himself, obviously thinking he'd blown it. One of the Old Bill asked, "Is this the lad who used the knife on you?" I looked at the lad who, like I said, was in a panic and said, "No, never seen him before. It definitely wasn't him." Then I added, "He wasn't even involved in the trouble." They released him and he was away as fast as he could go. The coppers let me keep the knife as a "memento" and off they went.

I sorted my leg out and was back on the main door when the lad who had stabbed me appeared again. "Can I have a word with you, mate?" he said. "Yeah, let's go out the back where it's quiet." When we got into the same back corridor, Mark came to see what was going on. The lad said how sorry he was and that he was made up that I didn't grass him. I told him, "I wouldn't have grassed you, no matter what. The thing is, if I gave you a kicking you wouldn't grass me up, would you?" I was leading him right up the garden path but he didn't know it. "Would you grass me?" I asked again. "No," he replied. "Whack!" I cracked him and put him straight on his arse, then immediately leapt on him and pounded his face. While I was doing this I pulled the knife out and held it to his face and said, "How would you like it if I stabbed you, ya little shit?" Our Mark was screaming at me, "Paul, fucking stab him." I thought about it, but a hiding was good enough for him. I climbed off him and gave him a few kicks for good measure and then threw him into the street. My own justice was more satisfying than if I had told the police it was him.

I didn't see the lad for a couple of years, then one night I was at a house party and he was there. The girl whose house it was caught him stealing something and I caught hold of him in the kitchen. The first thing that came to hand was a large, metal soup ladle, so I proceeded to smash his head with it. I wasn't worried, I knew he wouldn't grass me up. I never saw him again after that. He probably crosses the road when he sees me coming.

PIZZA MAN

WE NOT ONLY had some scary moments on the door, we got them elsewhere as well. I was in the house one day when my mate Greg from South Bank phoned. He sounded livid and told me that he'd had a bit of chew outside his house and two lads he was arguing with had threatened him and his wife, Louise, with a bread knife. I didn't know what the trouble was all about but I said I would be down as soon as possible.

I jumped in the car and on the way phoned our Mark, explaining what was going down. He told me to pick him up. When I got to my brother's house a lad called Marco, who worked in one of the local pizza shops, was with him and agreed to come too. I'd known Marco for around fifteen years, and he'd told me he came from Morocco and wanted to settle in Middlesbrough. He was quiet and seemed okay and was a normal run-of-the-mill lad. He'd met a local girl and had a kid to her, so he seemed pretty genuine. We grabbed a couple of bats and off we went to sort out the trouble.

We'd driven a couple of miles and were now heading into the South Bank area when my mobile rang. It was Greg. He'd told the lads that I was on my way down to sort them out, and apparently they were saying, "Wait until he gets here, he's gonna get this," and they were waving a large carving knife about. This only added fuel to the fire and I put my foot down to get there a bit quicker. When we pulled into Greg's road, everyone was out at the front of their houses. Greg's road was long and lined with houses with small front gardens and it looked like there was a Jubilee party or something going on. Everyone was at their gates and Greg said the ones we wanted had gone up to a house around the corner. Our kid and me had a bat each and Marco pulled out a large knife. I wasn't sure whether he would have used it or not, but at the time I couldn't care less.

As we got about thirty yards from this lad's house, the pair of them were leaning up against a Jeep of some sort and they didn't even flinch. Instead, one of them reached into his leather jacket and pulled out a handgun. He raised it in typical American cop style, pointed it straight at me and just stood still. The whole street was shouting for me to kill him but, bearing in mind he was pointing a gun straight at me, I stopped in my tracks and took stock of the situation. He still didn't move, nor did he say anything. In my experience, someone who is waving a knife or a gun, and shouting, "I'm gonna kill you," is the one who doesn't normally do it. It's the quiet ones who just pull the weapon on you that are the ones more likely to pull the trigger.

What seemed like ages but must have only been a couple of seconds passed and I said to him, "Put the gun down and we'll sort it out, one on one." He remained silent, still pointing the gun straight at me. His mate was holding a knife large enough to skin an elephant. Drastic action was needed. I was raging that this shitbag had pulled the gun on me, and wanted to do him in for his cheek. I looked down at my feet. There was a lot of rubble by the side of the road and I got my eye on a half house brick. I thought, if only I can get my hands on it before he fucking shoots me, I would be able to bounce it off his head.

Somebody shouted something further up the road and for a split second he took his eye off me. That was my chance. Quick as a flash, I dropped down, picked up the brick, and threw it at him as hard as I could. It whizzed past his ear with only an inch to spare. If it had hit him it would have taken his head off. Next thing he fired the gun and there was a loud crack and then smoke. For a split second I thought I was fucked, but nothing hit me. I ran straight at him and he and his mate both turned and ran up the path towards the house. My brother was quickly behind me, as was Marco the pizza man with his large knife.

I wasn't quick enough, because they reached the back door and ran inside. I could see through the frosted glass as he frantically locked the back door and I aimed the bat for his head through the window. The bat connected but just bounced off the window, cracking it. What I didn't know was that the window was reinforced in the middle with plastic. Lucky for him, I suppose, otherwise he would have been wearing the bat.

I ran to the front of the house where there was a large front room window. In the garden was a pile of paving slabs, which by now our kid was throwing, one by one, through the window, knocking out the glass and frame. The lad was now getting a new patio laid on his front room carpet. Everyone was shouting for us to kill them. Apparently these two weren't the most popular in the road. The bombardment of the paving stones went on for a couple of minutes until somebody shouted that the police were on their way; they'd heard it on a scanner radio, which intercepts the police airwaves.

We made our way back around the corner and into Greg's house. I was really pissed off that this lad had fired the gun at me, and I hadn't got my own back. We waited until the situation had quietened down and then got back in the car and fucked off away from the area.

We went back the next day but the lads involved had done one and gone missing. I knew I had been up for the situation and I knew Mark was, but I wasn't sure if Marco had been. I know he'd brought a knife with him but I didn't know whether he was bluffing or whether he would have used it. A couple of years later I would find out.

I'd been to work one day and decided to buy a local paper on the way home. When I looked at the front page I couldn't believe my eyes. On the front cover was a picture of Marco and the headline, "Serial murder suspect arrested." Marco was being held for three separate murders in Morocco. Apparently he'd stabbed three blokes to death in separate incidents, and then fucked off to England and ended up in Middlesbrough. He'd led a normal life for years and remained undetected. I thought to myself, thank fuck we didn't get our hands on those two lads, I'd have probably being doing life now.

So our local pizza man was a multiple murderer. It just goes to show, you never judge a book by its cover, not even mine. And next time you go to a pizza shop and you're pissed, don't set your lip up to the foreigner behind the counter. You never know...

SCAM OR BE SCAMMED

ANYONE WHO KNOWS me knows I love a scam. It's what makes the world go round. People used to phone me with some good scams and over the years I made some good money out of them. One particular scam was when one of my mates explained to me that he had been to his mate's garage, where they repaired cars, and he'd seen an old Porsche 911 there which was having a new rear valance fitted. My mate was told by his friend that the Porsche was a ringer, so he followed the driver home and watched where he parked it, a large, posh house in a nice part of town. My mate picked me up and I asked him how sure he was that the Porsche was a ringer. He was 100 per cent positive.

"Nice one" I said. "Show me where it is."

We drove to the address and parked just round the corner. When we approached the drive, an old Asian bloke cutting the grass asked what we wanted. "Where's the owner of the car?" I said. He looked at me, and I think at this point he decided he had forgotten how to speak English, like they do when they're put on the spot. I walked past him up to the front door and knocked. A couple of minutes passed and an Asian woman answered the door. I repeated the question and she smiled and said, "In here, I'll just get him."

Now we were getting somewhere. The lad came to the door and looked a bit puzzled. He didn't know us from Adam and he was probably wondering what this big fucker and his mate wanted.

"Is this your car, mate?" I said.

He looked even more puzzled and then he said, "Yeah, why, what's wrong?"

I said, "I'll tell you what's wrong, it's my fucking car."

He smiled and said, "No, you've got it wrong, I've got the log book and everything." I knew he was lying out of his arse, but we were going to soon see who was best, him at lying or me at bluffing.

"Listen mate," I went on, "I know it's my car. I can tell by the scuff on the front wing." I then walked to the rear of the car and said, "It's had a new rear valance fitted as well." I could see he was now panicking and I thought, ha! Fucking got you now.

I said, "What gives you the right to drive my car around?"

He was panicking now. "We can sort this out, mate," he said.

"Right," I replied, "You've got three choices. You can either give me the car back with the log book, and we will forget about it. Or, as I paid nine grand for the car but only got six back on insurance after it was stolen, you can give me the three grand difference and we'll forget about it. Or, I'll get the cops round now."

He stood and thought about what I had said and went for the second choice, the three grand. He told us that this place was his parents' house and gave us another address to come back to in an hour's time. We left and drove round for an hour. My mate who had put me on the scam was worried that the police would be waiting for us at the address he'd given us but I told him, "Don't be so fucking daft. If it's like you say it is and it's definitely a dodgy motor, then he's not likely to phone them, is he?"

We went to the address he'd given us and I suspected it might have been dodgy or there might be a squad of lads waiting for us, but to my surprise, there was the Porsche, parked outside. We knocked on the door and a very sheepish lad answered. "Come in lads," he said. We did. "Look mate, I can only give you a thousand this week, and the same next week and the same again the following week. But how do I know you won't phone the police on me when you've got your three grand?"

I assured him I wouldn't and we left his house a grand in pocket. I shared it with my mate and he said, "You're not going back next week, are you?"

"Fucking right I am."

He laughed, shook his head and pointed out I was off my head.

It was three weeks before Christmas when we got the first grand and we both returned the following two weeks to collect our money. As you can imagine, the timing was handy for presents.

Christmas Eve and I'm stood on the pub door working. It was a busy night and there were four of us. I turned round and who's walking towards me but the lad who'd given me the three grand.

"Alright mate," he said. "Everything okay?"

"Yeah, I'm okay," I said.

He then went on. "Do you know, mate, it's just cost me three grand three weeks before Christmas, and I'm skint."

He went on for ages, giving it the hard-done-by act. In the end he was pissing me off so much I turned and said, "You're not the brightest of people, are you?"

"What do you mean? I've just given you three grand, and I was going to ask you to buy me a drink for Christmas."

"Let me tell you something," I said. "It wasn't even my car you fucking halfwit. Don't you know when you've been had? Now fuck off and go and celebrate Christmas somewhere else."

His jaw hit the floor. He couldn't take in what I'd just told him and for a second I thought he was going start crying. He turned and walked away. The other three doormen were crying with laughter. They thought I was a cunt. A funny cunt, but a cunt nonetheless. Needless to say, I had a good Christmas and never saw the lad again. He probably went home and topped himself for being such a twat.

SELF DESTRUCTION

TOWARDS THE BACK end of the Nineties I went through a bad time. I was taking more drugs than I should have been. Things done in moderation don't do anybody any harm but I was never one for moderation. I always take things too far and this was no exception.

My wife at the time ended up moving back to her mother's and I was left to my own devices. I was home alone and hit the self-destruct button, not because she had left me, it was just that there was no one to bend my ear for doing what I was doing. I had a free rein. In a couple months, drugs were my priority instead of keeping myself right and sorting out situations.

I went from bad to worse. I stopped going to work and lost my job. My ex-wife was trying to get me out of the house and on to the streets and I had nowhere to go. She came to see me one day and told me I needed help and that she would take me to St. Luke's Hospital, a "nuthouse" where they deal with druggies and alcoholics, so I agreed to go, as she had booked me an appointment. We arrived and went into the reception area, where we were told where to go and were escorted through a load of doors that were unlocked and then locked again behind us.

Now, I'm no Einstein but I knew something was wrong. When

we reached the office on the ward where I had the appointment, I was told to wait. I sat there with my ex-wife and she was telling me things would be OK and that I would only have to stay for a few days or a week at most. I looked around and saw one lad talking to himself in a chair in the corner and somebody else rocking back and forth in another chair. *One Flew Over the Cuckoo's Nest* came to mind.

When I went in to see the shrink he explained to me that I had to sign my name and the treatment for my drug habit would start straight away. I paused for a while. I know I've been called mad before and I've got a few slates missing, but I'm no window licker and I quickly realised they were trying to section me. It dawned on me that her plan was to get me sectioned and then she would get the house, car, everything, and I'd be left playing with my imaginary friends like a right ding.

"Sorry mate," I said, "Do I look fucking backward?"

I got up and said, "You'd better get this fucking door unlocked now."

He apologised to my ex-wife and explained that I had to either be sent to the hospital by the courts or admit myself. Fuck that for a laugh. I left the hospital still with a bad drug habit and I thought I'd rather be free and on drugs than locked up with the proper loons. I saw the look on my ex-wife's face; I'd fucked up her plan. Sorry. She had to go back to the drawing board. I went back to the house and she went back to her mother's.

I spent another couple of weeks in the house and then I was ordered out by a court on the grounds I was a danger to her and that I would kill her. I would have been out of jail by now if I had. My relationship was down the tubes big time. It had been for years. I'd been seeing a lass who lived just around the corner for the previous couple of years, so I suppose it had been over a long time. This girl wanted me to make a commitment to her before I went apeshit on the drugs, and at one time I nearly did. She became pregnant to me but miscarried and lost the baby. I was quite close to this girl so I was gutted for her. I couldn't believe I had got away with seeing her for so long without getting my cover blown, because at the time everyone seemed to know about it. She even came round the house from time to time when I was alone and stayed the afternoon, so I was surprised that the neighbours never said anything.

I ended up in bed-sit land, an area in Middlesbrough full of prostitutes and junkies. I spent a year living down there, went through some horrendous times and did some horrible things to people. I won't go into the details. I could write another book about it. But in the end, I was left with nothing.

I'd just come out of hospital after spending a couple of weeks there for an incident involving too many drugs and was at an all-time low. I had fuck-all and, to be honest, I thought I was finished. Everyone had me written off but one person, my old friend Greg, and his wife Louise, stood by me throughout my ordeal. They invited me to live with them until I got myself sorted. I moved in and they helped me get myself back on my feet again. After six or seven weeks, I was looking and feeling normal again.

I started weight training once more in a gym close by and the owner, Mark, told me he wanted to see me back to my old self and that I could train for free until I was sorted. You find out who your friends are when you're really down. Some people didn't want to know me when I was low, not that I was looking for sympathy or freebies or anything. Most of how I was at this time was self-inflicted anyway.

I started training on a regular basis and didn't touch any drugs and was soon starting to feel back to my old self. I left Greg's house, got myself a council flat in South Bank and was soon getting back on my feet. I used a local shop on a regular basis and I knew a girl who worked there. I had known her for years but had never really spoken to her. We became quite friendly and I asked her out. The girl in question, Elaine, knew what I had just been through, so I was surprised when she said yes.

We seemed to hit it off straight away. She had her own place, own car, and was a brilliant laugh. We went out on a regular basis and were getting on so well that, after a couple of months, I gave up my flat and moved in with her. I was on my way back up and earning good money doing a few dodgy deals but I needed a bit of stability in my life. I needed a job, a regular income, so I applied for a job working offshore and landed it. This was the turning point for me; it gave me back my independence and, with a regular income, I could do the things I had missed out on for a couple of years.

I'd been with Elaine for around five months when we took a holiday to Acapulco, Mexico. While there, she told me that six months before I asked her out she had been to see a fortune teller who had written down her future. She showed it to me. It read, "You will meet someone in the future that you have known for years and this person will become your soul mate. He will be dressed in black on your first date and be a gentle giant." When I first took Elaine out I wore black trousers, a black top and black jacket. She said she nearly fell over when she saw what I was dressed in. The fortune teller went on to say, "You will go on holiday with this person to an American country and within two years you will buy a house with this person and have a child." Everything the fortune teller said has come true. Not sure about the gentle giant bit though. I normally don't believe in all that shite but I've read these predictions and to be honest it's scary. Pity she didn't predict we were going to win the Lottery but, looking back, I hit the jackpot anyway when I met Elaine.

SELF DESTRUCTION

I started going back to the matches and we had a few offs but now the whole scene is fucked. It makes me laugh because you have two sets of lads in the street wanting the same thing. It happens and the courts absolutely hammer us with banning orders and jail sentences. I received a two-year custodial sentence in 1984, as you have read. Okay, I admit the circumstances were bad but I was only charged with an affray. If you're a paedophile and mess about with kids you are more than likely to get a slapped wrist. It's only when they get a serial paedophile with umpteen charges that they actually jail them, and then they only get eighteen months or something similar. Fucking eighteen months for child abuse, I would set the dirty cunts on fire; even that's too good for them.

We bought a house together around three years ago and shortly afterwards got the news we'd been waiting for: Elaine was pregnant. We were both over the moon and when she had the baby it was a little boy, Tommy. They are the best thing that has happened to me. I've come a long way from those drugs days in a short space of time and I tend to behave myself from now on.

I have been to a few matches in the past couple of years but you can't do shit now without the Old Bill breathing down your neck, so, in short, I've retired. People encouraged me to write this book and the process brought back a lot of memories and put me back in touch with people I haven't seen for years. We talked about the good old days when everyone used to run wild on a Saturday afternoon up and down the country, especially the Eighties scene.

Nothing will ever change what went on in those days and it will never be the same. After two decades of being a hooligan I saw many changes, some crazy fashions and haircuts in the early days, right through the Northern Soul scene and wraps of speed, and into the rave and 'E' scene. Nowadays some lads think being a football hooligan is a fashion statement. They wear the clothes and that makes them a hooligan. In the early days we were hooligans first and the fashion just came with it.

What makes me laugh, too, is the hooligan websites you log on to. People having cyber arguments about who has done what and who ran away. Some of the posts are constructive and I could always tell which people were genuine and had been there and who were the wannabes. So to all you cyber warriors out there, for fuck's sake, get a life. If you didn't do it when you had the chance, tough shit. Some of them sit there giving it the big 'un in the safety of their homes. Where were they when it mattered and it was backs-to-the-wall time?

ME AND MOTORCYCLES – A BAD COMBINATION

MOTORBIKES AND ME just don't mix. I found this out the hard way but I always did find out things the hard way. I just don't do "easy".

Back in the mid-Nineties, for some strange reason I decided I wanted a superbike. I hadn't even ridden one before but I thought it couldn't be that hard and it looked fun, so I applied to do a Direct Access course to pass my bike test so I could buy any size bike I wanted. It consisted of a three-day course with my test at the end of it. I started off weaving around cones on a moped and it was a piece of piss. We moved up to a 500cc bike and two days later I was sitting my test. I passed straight away and was buzzing like fuck. I went straight out and bought a Yamaha 600 Thundercat Sport, capable of around 150mph. I got togged up with all the leathers, gloves, boots, the full issue, and thought I was the next Barry Sheene.

I had had the bike a couple of months and my mate Phil, who had been riding bikes for years, told me there was a ride out on the following Sunday when more than seventy bikes would be leaving Middlesbrough and riding up to Hemsley and then on to

THE BRICK

Pickering. The Hemsley-Pickering route is well known as a perfect biker's road, full of sweeping bends through the countryside.

I met Phil at his house and we rode into the town centre and met up with all the others going out that day. It was a beautiful sunny day, perfect for biking. The more experienced bikers were racing up at the front and, by the time we were a couple of miles outside Middlesbrough, I was with them. I was keeping up with them, no problem, but my combination of too much bottle and too little experience was going to prove dangerous. As we raced down the country lanes, through the sweeping bends, I was riding like a maniac. I was overtaking more experienced lads with ease and I can remember thinking to myself, piece of piss, this. I was doing well over 100mph and I was actually riding quite well, apart from a slight brush with a BMW coming the other way. I was the first to pull into Hemsley Square with the rest of the pack behind me. Phil, my mate, said that that I had ridden brilliantly and he couldn't believe I had only been biking for such a short time. Because I had ridden so well on the way to Hemsley I thought I was invincible. I couldn't have been more wrong.

Just before we left Hemsley to set off for Pickering, I said to Phil, "Let's hang back for ten minutes and let everyone else set off and we'll have a bit of fun overtaking them." He agreed, so we waited and then set off in hot pursuit and had a whale of a time whizzing past them all when we came to a slight uphill climb along a long straight road. There were quite a few cars both in our lane and oncoming so we were going in between the cars up the white lines. I caught up to a lad on a Honda Fireblade who was also going in between the cars. As I raced up behind him I looked at the speedo and I was doing around 90mph.

He suddenly braked, so I grabbed my front brake and squeezed. My front wheel locked up and I was catapulted straight over the handlebars and into the air. I flew through the air thinking, oh, shit, this is gonna hurt, and landed on my hip. I bounced along, cartwheeling, for about fifty yards, whacking my arms and legs on the tarmac. The bike did a couple of somersaults and then slid straight under an oncoming car and it and the car were written off. I didn't hit anything apart from the ground and slid to a stop.

Phil, who was behind me, later said he thought I was dead and got the shock of his life when I just stood straight up and took off my helmet. There were bits of bike everywhere but I didn't even have a broken bone. I was in full leathers and I firmly believe they saved me from any serious injury. An ambulance came within minutes but I told them I was okay.

Actually, I started to go into shock and went a ghastly shade of white. I didn't want to go to hospital, so one of the lads went home on his bike and came back in his van to pick up me and my bike. We loaded what was left of the bike into the van and on the way home I was so sore I changed my mind and decided to get checked out at the hospital. They X-rayed me from head to foot and told me nothing was broken but I had deep bruising to my legs and hips. I had a drip in my arm and the leathers I had been wearing were in a right mess on the floor next to my bed.

I phoned my brother to bring me some clothes, as they told me I had to stay in under observation. When he arrived, the curtain was around my bed. He came through and asked if I was okay. I said, "Yeah, course I am," and promptly pulled the drip out of my arm, got dressed and did one out of the hospital. Fuck knows what the nurses must have thought when they discovered I had disappeared, but I was more bothered about my bike, so off I went.

A couple of weeks later I had a new bike; an even bigger one this time. It lasted about eight weeks and then it was written off. Gravity doesn't seem to like me.

A short while later my mate Greg's wife, Louise, went to see a fortune teller who asked her, "Do you know someone with a motorbike, a big lad with dark hair?" Louise said, "Yes, it's Paul you're talking about." The fortune teller warned, "Tell him to never ever get on a motorbike ever again. Not even as a passenger." As soon as Louise told me this, it was the end of bikes and me. Don't get me wrong, I would love another bike, but that might be tempting fate.

ENGLAND v. TURKEY
Stadium of Light, Sunderland

WHEN IT WAS announced that England were to play Turkey at the Stadium of Shite in Sunderland, everyone thought this was going to be World War Three. The Press had hyped it up for weeks before the game, saying there were going to be repercussions for the Turks because they had stabbed and killed two Leeds United fans in Turkey. Half the time the Press is to blame for the trouble, hyping the game up and whipping up a frenzy in the papers for weeks before the fixture. I know lads who have been into Europe with England, and when it's about to go off, television reporters have said, "Go on lads, get stuck in," just so they can report that the English are hooligans. How bad is that? They tell them to kick off, then call them hooligans.

Anyway, leading up to this game we decided to take a large mob. After all, it was happening in the North East, where we're from, so we had to represent ourselves as best we could. Most of our lads had tickets for this one, including me, and we decided to stay away from Middlesbrough town centre and instead just stay in our own local boozers, keep in touch by mobile, and then amass in Sunderland. The idea was to send four lads up in a taxi;

THE BRICK

Sunderland is only about forty miles from Middlesbrough, so taxis were the order of the day. They were told to find a boozer in Sunderland centre, phone home, and then in fours we would all arrive separately at the same boozer, so avoiding detection. Our plan worked brilliantly and, as the last taxi arrived we were all safely in the boozer, and there was well over 150 of us.

We expected the Sunderland mob to show up and we would have had it with them, but apparently they were drinking on the other side of town, or so they said. We had been in there a couple of hours, wondering what was going to go off, when this lad walked in on his own and, of all the people to walk over to, he came over to me.

"Does anyone want any coke?" he asked.

I thought to myself, you fucking ding. But I replied, "I'll just ask the lads."

I had a word and told him we wanted six grams, so off he went, proud as fuck, thinking he was about to make a few quid. I didn't think for one minute he'd come back and when he did he must have had a few slates missing, because he said to me, "Come in the toilets mate, I've got what you want." I nearly fell over laughing. So in we went.

"Here you are, mate," he said, and promptly handed over six bags of coke. "Forty pounds a gram," he said. "That's two hundred and forty quid."

"Yeah, right ho mate. Catch you later."

I turned round and dished out a gram to the lads I was with, who were now falling about laughing. Did he get paid? Stop asking silly questions. He was tortured for being a ding. I mean, 150 lads in a pub and he asked me. He couldn't have asked a worse person, but he learned a lesson.

It was nearing seven o'clock now, and we were enjoying the day. Who wouldn't? Plenty of drink, free coke, so we decided to make our move. We had heard Newcastle were bringing a massive mob, as you'd expect as it's only eight miles from Sunderland, but they didn't show. Apparently they were intercepted on their way and all turned back because they didn't have tickets. It was a shame really. We'd have had a drink with them... NOT!

We'd have turned anybody over that night, but it wasn't to be. There was a massive police presence. We'd walked a short distance when we came to a social club on the left hand side of the road. The doors opened and a few Sunderland lads came out, shouting abuse. I remember a fat twat with a Stone Island jumper on largeing it at the front. I caught him with a cracking right hand and sent him tumbling backwards.

"We're England," he said. Where had I heard that before?

"And we're fucking Boro," I said,

Just then, out of the corner of my eye I saw a riot cop coming at me. He hit me straight across the thigh with his baton. The pain was immense, but he didn't try to arrest me, he just pushed me away and told me to fuck off.

"Nice one, mate. I'll fuck off as quick as you like."

We were swamped by police. They were everywhere, and you could hear the helicopter above us. I've never seen so many coppers.

We walked towards the ground and we thought we might bump into another mob along the way. When we came to the Wheatsheaf pub, there was a mob of Hull. One of their lads came forward and was promptly poleaxed in the middle of the road. He must have been fucked because when I looked back he was in the recovery position and two coppers were tending to him. Unlucky mate – learn to block.

When we arrived at the ground the police were well pissed off with us and steamed us with batons drawn. Then the Turks' coaches arrived and their attention was diverted from us to them.

Loads of English fans attacked the coaches and even tried to open the doors. The Turks must have been shitting themselves. We stood near the turnstiles and watched what was happening. Lots of people were getting nicked. My leg was throbbing from the whack with the baton and later, when I looked at it, I had a beauty go-faster stripe right across my thigh. Mind you, I'd sooner be whacked with a baton than be locked up, any day of the week.

Throughout the match there was a pretty hostile atmosphere. Everyone loves the Turks, though, don't they? Half-time came and we were in the concourse, and I was spotted by several police football intelligence officers. "Now then, Mr. Debrick. What are you doing here, blah, blah, blah?" I thought, I can't go anywhere. In the end everywhere I went I was picked out every time. That's why I stopped going.

After the game we left together and made our way back to Sunderland city centre, but the plod had it well sussed and there was no chance of a kick-off . We boarded a train to Darlington, where we would get a drink outside the station, but when we arrived a large number of police immediately attacked us with batons and dogs. They had been waiting for us and took no shit. People were now splitting up and it was definitely time for a sharp exit. Four of us piled into a taxi and fucked off straight away. I figured that if I stayed I would have been locked up, so off we went.

It was not a bad day really, but would have been better if more had made a show. I had a bruise on my leg for days after and was walking like a gimp for a week.

COMPETITION TIME

IN THE SUMMER of 2003 I was bang into my training again and was lifting weights like they were going out of fashion. I had been following a strict diet and was thinking of competing in a bodybuilding show. My partner, Elaine, said, "Go for it."

We went to the North Britain show, a local qualifier for the British bodybuilding finals, just to see what the set up was like and establish if I was going to go for this one a year later. Elaine had never been to a bodybuilding show before and was amazed at the quality of competition. She gave me her full backing and told me to go ahead and she would help me in anyway she could.

Mark, who owns my local gym, Body Talk Health and Fitness, told me I could train for free because I would be representing his establishment, so, over the moon, I threw myself head-first into a punishing regime that lasted for a year. Nelly, a local lad who used to compete, and his brother, Gav, both helped me with my diet and guided me through the final steps of my preparation.

As the months passed and I got into better shape, I decided I would do a sixteen-week pre-contest diet, which consisted of eating just chicken breasts, egg whites, baked potatoes and plenty of veg. The training was the easy bit; it's the part I enjoyed most. The diet side was the hardest. I like to burn the candle at both ends and I like a night out, but I had to put all this on hold whilst trying to get into shape. I trained with weights every day, did cardiovascular work in the mornings and then again in the evening. At first, the whole diet thing was bland and boring but, as the body fat dropped off and I saw myself becoming lean, I started to enjoy it. And the better shape I developed, the more determined I became.

I was on course for the competition in September 2004 when disaster struck. I had been taking steroid shots to hold the muscle tissue while I was dieting and I got an infection in my thigh. I first noticed a small lump on my right thigh, which was very sore. After a couple of days it became quite large and I started to limp. A couple of more days and I decided that the doctor was the best port of call. He confirmed that I had an infection and prescribed a course of antibiotics. They didn't even touch the infection and, within a few more days, my thigh was like a balloon and I was in absolute agony. In the end, Elaine took me to hospital. A surgeon examined me and told me I needed immediate surgery.

He said, "If you don't, the pressure in your thigh will stop the circulation and you could lose your leg."

"Lose my fucking leg?" I was shocked.

They took me straight down to theatre and when I came to I was told they had taken 600 millilitres of poison out of my thigh; that's more than a pint. I was gob-smacked at what he was telling me. He went on, "And we have had to leave an open wound right down to the bone and it has to heal from the inside out." I was gutted. I had been training solid for a long time for this show. I had been dieting for ten weeks and had put in so much time, money and effort, and sacrificed so much. Everyone told me it was over and there was no way I would compete in six weeks time. At the time, I viewed this as a major setback, but I wasn't to be beaten by it. I was down but I wasn't out and it just made me more determined to compete.

The next morning I awoke in hospital and told the nurse I wanted a bath. "No problem," she said, "but you will have to take the packing out of the hole in your leg and then we will repack it for you." As I walked into the bathroom my leg felt fine; with all the poison now gone there was no pressure in my thigh and no pain at all. I removed the bandage and saw a hole in my thigh about three inches long and two inches wide. It had little strips of wadding hanging out of it and I knew I had to take it all out. "Here we go," I thought, and started pulling out the packing. It was like a magician pulling handkerchiefs out from a hat, it went on forever. In the end there was a huge pile of wadding on the floor and I was left with a dirty great hole in my thigh, the size of an elephant's fanny. They repacked it for me and off I went, limping.

I was back in the gym two days later but all I could train was my upper body. My leg training had gone down the pan but I was determined to compete. I was quite surprised at how quickly my leg was healing and I got on course to prove everyone wrong. The last four weeks of the diet were a nightmare and I starved all day, trying to drop the body fat. Elaine prepared all my meals and encouraged me all the way. Even when I wanted to stray from my diet and pig out, she kept me on the straight and narrow and helped me through the hunger pangs.

In the last week or so I saw Nelly and Gav every day and they helped me enormously. Competition day came and it was time to put all the hard work, training and diet into action and I travelled to Durham for the show. I thought I would be nervous but I enjoyed every minute of it. I wasn't in the top three, but I wasn't disappointed at all. I had come back from being on the streets and totally fucked on drugs, to a competition-level bodybuilder. I was pleased with how I looked, and Elaine said I did myself proud.

THE BRICK

The photograph of me in this book shows I was in the best shape of my life. Not bad for a bloke of forty, eh? I am seriously considering competing again in the over-forties line-up but it takes a lot of time, effort and dedication, so who knows? Now I am just happy training and keeping myself in shape. I suppose I will always train, it's second nature and I love the buzz.

HOOLIGANISM
THEN AND NOW

AS SOON AS I was introduced to football violence, just by accident, I loved every minute of it. In those early days you didn't get all the high-tech surveillance that you do now, and there were no police Football Intelligence Units. We went all over the country in those early Eighties days, as most mobs did, totally undetected. Lads would go into the city centres and rob the shops of designer gear, drink, fight, and generally go berserk.

Back in my shoplifting days, when we went away to football we would suss out all the top shops in different cities or smaller towns, then we would return days later to steal from them. These days most of the football lads have good jobs and plenty of money, so they can afford to buy their Prada or Stone Island, C.P. Company and so on. We had fuck all in those early days – no jobs, no cash, so if we wanted to be decked out in designer gear we had to nick it.

It's funny, because we'd be up and down the country nicking Farah trousers and Pierre Cardin and Lyle and Scott jumpers. At the time, if you had Farah trousers you were smart as fuck. Wouldn't do the garden in them now. If I did have money I'd get the train to Manchester on my own and go to a little shop called Oasis, which wasn't even a real proper shop. Everyone in the know knew this is where you could get your top trainers from, when nobody else stocked them.

I got my first pair of Trimm Trabb from there. I thought I was the bees knees when I went to my next match wearing them These days lads don't travel like we did to quench our desire for designer gear. When all the tennis gear was in, we'd go to the tennis centres, which were a soft touch, and come home wearing new Fila and Tacchini. Some of our lads even went to these tennis centres with tennis rackets in their hands so to blend in with the members. Good thinking, eh?

We played Derby County in the very early Eighties and right in the centre was a sports shop which sold Lacoste, Fila, and the like. We piled in and stole most of the tracksuits, then went straight to the Post Office and posted them home. A short while later the plod arrived and we were searched but nobody had anything on them, so they let us go. They must have been scratching their heads.

Anyway, back to the fighting side of things. We'd turn up in cities at 11am, just in time for the pubs to open, and you could choose to go where you wanted without any hassle from the Old Bill. They rarely even came to a pub unless there was an off, so you could get away with a lot more then than you could now. We didn't have all this Internet stuff and mobile phone arrangements but we had much better fights than in recent years. Those of you old enough to remember those good old days will know exactly what I'm talking about and it will probably kindle a few good memories. Football violence wasn't just a Saturday thing, you lived it every day; it was a way of life.

As we moved into the Nineties, CCTV in the city centres became commonplace, which made it harder for the would-be hooligan. You see, without cameras or Football Units it was happy days, but with technology moving along at a fast pace, lads were now thinking twice about football, it was so easy to get nicked.

In the mid-Nineties I used to go to a few select away games and then lay low for a while. It got ridiculous in the end. A handful of us would turn up at King's Cross around 10am and Plod would be waiting for us with camcorders. I've lost count of the number of times I've arrived in a different place, and as soon as I got off the train their Police Intelligence picked me out and it was, "Now then, Mr. Debrick, where are you heading?" I couldn't go anywhere, and as I was becoming known everywhere I used to leave it for a while, then return when I thought I was out of the limelight. Mind you, I didn't exactly blend in, in the mid-Nineties I was about eighteen and a half stone and six feet one; not your average football hooligan, but a formidable one.

Our own Police Intelligence were now on first-name terms with nearly all our top lads, and would come into the pubs and bring the opposing team's Intelligence officers in. As John Theone said in his book *The Frontline*, "Somebody must have been loose with their lips, because we'd turn up just outside a strange city, on the outskirts, waiting to make our move and, you guessed it, Intelligence would turn up. They turned up just at the right time, and so most of the time our plans were down the pan."

In June 2003, shortly before an England match, I received a letter from Cleveland Police:

Dear Mr Debrick
The European Championship football fixture between England and Slovakia will take place at the Riverside Stadium, Middlesbrough, in Wednesday, 11th June, 2003. I am writing to inform you of the preparations I am making in order to prevent violence and disorder in the Cleveland Police area.

At this time I have reasonable grounds to believe that football related disorder is likely to occur in connection with this fixture. I believe that if preventative action is not taken, the result would be violence and disorder within Cleveland and especially in and around the Riverside Stadium and town centre of Middlesbrough.

You have come to Police notice owing to your actions and/ or associations involving football related disorder. In order to prevent violence and disorder, I must warn you that you will be liable to arrest should you be in the Cleveland Police area in circumstances which it is believed you are likely to participate in violence and disorder

If you are prosecuted for a football related offence you may face a custodial sentence. In addition, an application will be made to the court for a Football Banning Order under the Football (Disorder) Act 2000. Such an order would prevent you from attending both domestic and international football matches for a minimum period of three years.

Yours sincerely

D Lumb

Chief Superintendent

Middlesbrough

These letters, and the banning orders themselves, are becoming the norm now for one-time football lads, even some who haven't been in a fight for twenty years. You can get them just for *knowing* the wrong people. Guilt by association; great, isn't it?

I think the odds are stacked against the would-be football hooligan now. They use everything in their power to stop it and most of our top lads are already under the dreaded banning orders, so they don't bother anymore. I'll probably get a ban myself when they read this book. It's almost inevitable, even though I haven't been for a couple of years they will still ban me because they have to be seen to be doing something. Anyway, ban me, like I give a fuck. What you should have done is ban me twenty-odd years ago, but you're not that quick. A ban now would only mean that I couldn't go to somewhere that I stopped going to a couple of years ago, anyway. If that makes sense. Pointless, really, but I'll have one anyway. I don't want to feel left out.

In my twenty-odd years of running with the mob I've witnessed many stabbings, slashings, beatings, you name it, I've seen it. Does it make me feel ashamed or bad at what I've done you may ask? No, not really. What's happened has happened. I can't change that. It was a big part of my life for so long. In fact for many years it was a way of life.

A lot of you will know what I'm talking about when you read this book, and you'll be able to relate to the things I write about. Some of you will probably be shocked at what I've written. If you are then the next book you read should be *The Beano*. I haven't set out to shock or glorify anything, it's just an honest account of my life with nothing hidden, or left out.

I don't want anybody to go and do what I've done over the years. This book is not supposed to inspire anybody to cause violence. What else can I say? Don't try this at home.

HATE US OR RATE US?

I THOUGHT IT would be interesting to get comments from lads from a variety of different clubs, big and small, to see what they think of Boro. Hate us or rate us, you can see from the views below that we always left an impression.

Carl Spiers from Oldham, author of the excellent, *We Are The Famous Football Hooligans*

In November, 1986, Oldham played Middlesbrough at Boundary Park in a Second Division game. I had not been active for a few years on the hooligan front and had spent most Saturdays playing amateur football, but I still ventured to Boundary Park. This day at about 2.30pm, I was making my way through the Chaddy End (Oldham's kop) when a mob of 100 Boro fans came charging across the terraces. Oldham's mob came down from the back of the stand to meet them head on. I felt I was going to be trapped in this melee and wanted no part of it, so I ducked under a crush barrier to try to get away, but I got trapped underneath with my head sticking out.

Boro got the upper hand and most Oldham fled, leaving me stuck under this barrier. It is then I received the first of dozens of boots and kicks in my face and head from Boro fans, it went on for a couple of minutes; I was kicked to fuck. I was unconscious and was stretchered around the perimeter of the pitch. I came round in the nearby hospital, where I was told I had a broken nose, a broken cheekbone, stitches around my eyes, a front tooth knocked out, plus severe bruising on my face and my head. My head had swollen to twice its normal size. I was kept in hospital for three days before being released. It was my worst ever kicking at a football match, and I had been fighting at the match for over ten years by that time.

Apparently Oldham fans regrouped and forced this Boro mob out of the Chaddy End and attacked them after the match as they approached their coaches. I will have to take their word. I did not feel any bitterness towards Middlesbrough at all; I put it down to losing my instincts at the match. I had been involved in hundreds of similar situations and very rarely came unstuck apart from a few bloody noses and bruises, plus I had always respected Boro as hooligan firm, they have taken on all the big boys and no-one took liberties up there.

A Leicester City lad

I was only a nipper when in 1987 we won at Ayresome Park on the last day of the season to stop them going up, though they eventually went up after beating Chelsea in the play-off, the one with the mass pitch invasion at the Bridge. City were locked in the ground for a good couple of hours as the police couldn't or wouldn't clear the angry locals. The Baby Squad were very active at the time but had little or no interest in getting out until OB had sorted it!

A Newcastle gadgy

Ayresome park was a fucking horrible place to get to, either from the train station, or otherwise. It went off every time at the station and along any route you chose to get to the ground. It was, all in all, a fucking nightmare of a place. It was like you were fighting your old man's mates, they always seemed twenty years older. Sanitised version at the Riverside though.

Boro are mental. FACT.

A Leeds veteran

I remember the away fans used to be in the Clive Road corner. Had fuckin' everything thrown at us. Leeds took a bit of a hiding one game in the Seventies; Ayresome Park was one dodgy place to go. Another time we were squashed into that bastard cage they had for away fans in the early Eighties on Bonfire Night (ish) and the fuckers were firing rockets at us

A Villa lad

Gotta say Boro is one horrible place to go, although you went knowing your were gonna get some great fun. I remember leaving once on a mild Saturday morning in T-shirts and when we got there it was fucking snowing. Doing the conga as the Boro fans were singing, "You're gonna get your fucking heads kicked." Ayresome Park sorted the men from the boys.

Arsenal lad 1

It was a cup game, can't remember the exact year but someone reckons it was '77, and Malcolm MacDonald was playing for us. Arsenal had sunk pretty low in the terrace ratings by then, but we did manage to take a reasonable crew up there. I went with a couple of others round to the Boro end, just in time to see nine or ten Arsenal going in. We followed quickly and ran up the steps. By the time we got up to join them, they had steamed into the Boro fans. It was about forty-five minutes before kick-off and the

Boro end was about three-quarters full. I kid you not, there were thousands of Boro, and not one of them stood. The whole lot of them ran and the end virtually emptied.

The police got us onto the pitch perimeter and walked us up to the away enclosure. What we hadn't realised was that all Boro's top boys had gone in the opposite end anyway, to try to get at the Arsenal fans. When we got down there, a few Arsenal spilled over the wall to join us and try to get in amongst Boro's main mob, but we had no chance. Boro had some game lads, and they were well up for it, they were never going to back off. The OB put us in among the Arsenal fans, and that was it, game over. The OB put up a screen between the fans to try and stop the hail of missiles being thrown, but not before an Arsenal fan had copped a dart right in his eyeball. We got murdered on the pitch, about 4-1 or similar. Lots of running battles on the way back to the station with honours about even, we took some bad injuries, but they were not totally unscathed either, we certainly didn't get smashed, although I've got to admit that we've had better days. I remember reading later that doctors saved the lad's eyesight.

Arsenal lad 2

Funny thing, I've met Arsenal who have classed the day as bit of a result and others like myself got battered and see it different. I went up by coach with a small group from my old school, at least four of us maybe more. I'd been away to Ipswich, Norwich, Coventry, Notts County, so thought I knew all there was to know about away games.

Got to the ground and while outside just watched the older Arsenal chasing off any Boro that came near. Got in the ground and just couldn't believe how the handful of Arsenal cleared the home end so easy. Boro looked like complete wankers. Arsenal seemed to be taking the piss. There was a good firm of Boro next to us in the corner but the Arsenal in with them seemed to be doing okay. Some poor sod jumped over the fence to join the rest of the Arsenal and caught his trousers on the top of the fence, ripping them from ankle to bollocks.

Can't remember much about the game except we were rubbish. When their fourth goal went in, a group of about 100 of us made our way outside. After what I'd seen earlier I thought we'd walk all over them. We strolled up towards the home end and into a fucking big mob which came from nowhere. Don't think they'd been in the ground. We got run everywhere.

We got hit from behind, in front and both sides. Ended up totally lost. I was kicked all over the place. I was shitting myself and worried that the coach would go with out me. More through luck than anything else we walked into the Arsenal mob heading to the station and walked with them back to the coaches.

A Bournemouth lad

We only ever played them once, got chased off before the game. Luckily it was snowing and they couldn't really be bothered. After the game we hid till they fucked off! If you've ever been in a motor with steamed up window surrounded by dozens of thugs, hoping they don't notice you, you will have an idea of what we were feeling. Scary fuckers, I thought.

An Oxford United lad

In the old days, before segregation, they came in our end and had a right go a couple of times. In one year in the early Seventies they had a right bunch of meatheads. They came in the London Road End tooled up with darts, snooker balls, I even remember two fellas with wooden mallets! They got pushed back – we were very handy then and had the numbers – but they were rough fuckers, no messing.

Been up there a few times, Ayresome and the new place, and strangely enough never had any bother, although you always got the feeling it was never far away, particularly at Ayresome Park.

One of the better firms over the years, and one thing I particularly like about the place is that they mostly support the Boro, you don't see kids running around in Man Utd shirts like you do in many other places. Pompey is another place like that, quite insular I suppose.

A Northampton lad

We haven't played them for years, as we have languished in the lower leagues for so long, but the many times I have been with them on England duties I have to say they one of the top three in the country, all big fuckers and game as they come. I would rate them head and shoulders above your Cardiffs of this world.

A Barnsley boy

I have always rated Boro as a firm, although they used blades on our mob when we travelled up their in the Eighties, that loses them some respect. I have come across their mob on a number of occassions, both in Barnsley and Manchester, and they always travel well. Barnsley have a bit of an history with Boro, and we have fronted each other at a few games. I also saw them when they more than held their own in Deansgate against Manchester United.

All in all a good firm and have been for years, but let themselves down that once when we visited and the knives were pulled.

WHY?

Some people have asked me why I did what I did for so long. Why I was a football hooligan, and what did I get out of it? It is very difficult to explain to people who have not been in the situation themselves. I was a football hooligan for a number of reasons, the adrenalin rush, the crack with the lads, and probably just going out for the day and getting off my face. All these reasons go hand in hand and make an away day complete.

I was a football hooligan for most of my adult life. Once, after I had been jailed for two years for football violence, I was asked, "Has it put you off?" The honest truth is, no, it didn't. All the way through my sentence I couldn't wait to get back to the games. After all, when I was inside in the mid-Eighties, hooliganism was at its height. It was rife throughout Britain and Europe and was a big part of my life. Like I have already said, being a football casual or hooligan was a way of life, not just a Saturday thing. A state of mind, if you like.

Every time I was arrested and either jailed or fined, I saw it as a minor setback and returned to my way of life straight away. People often call the likes of me mindless thugs, people who turn up on a Saturday afternoon and smack just about anybody, but as most of you already know, apart from the odd thick cunt, football firms are made up of some quite clever and bright individuals. Some of the organisation and planning that goes into some of it is quite sophisticated, especially when lads are trying to stay one step ahead of the plod. Nowadays, the police seem to be winning the battle against the hooligan, but with all the technology at their fingertips they're bound to. I look back now and I see my association with the darker side of football as an addiction; a drug, if you like, and like any junkie you need that fix.

In the Nineties I stopped going for a while and could stay away from it for a couple of months at a time but, I always craved the buzz, and when the lure of a big game came around, where I knew there was likely to be an off, I returned.

Once, when I'd had a few months off, the lure of an away fixture at Leeds tempted me out of my temporary layoff. We travelled by train and for some reason or another we lost our mob. Four of us were in the city centre on our own, and we received a phone call from our lads saying that they had gone to a boozer across the other side of the city. We took a taxi, which pulled up at some traffic lights. It was around noon, and people were going about their normal business.

As I glanced to my left I saw a massive Leeds mob come out of a boozer. They were obviously on the move. We were stuck at the lights so weren't going anywhere, and the mob was approaching the road to cross over, when I said to the lads in the taxi with me, "Shall we get out here?" The lads laughed and, to be honest, must have thought I was mad, because I jumped out of the passenger seat, stood straight in front of them and said, "Come on then, you daft cunts." To my surprise they clocked me and backed off. It was one of the funniest sights I've witnessed. The taxi driver was shitting himself and probably thought he was going to get his taxi wrecked. The lads I was with were cracking up laughing and shouted, "For fuck's sake, get back in the taxi."

WHY?

As I turned and climbed back in the cab, the lights turned green and the taxi slowly pulled off. It was then the Leeds mob realised that there were only four of us and started running after the taxi. Let's face it, I was on my own outside the cab and they could have killed me, but not one of them came at me. But as soon as they knew we were driving away they ran forward. Typical Leeds. When you read this book, Leeds, all I can say is you know what I think about your mob, and you had your chance that day. You should have kicked me to fuck but you were too slow, so go away and kick yourselves, it'll save me a job. I got a proper buzz from the situation I'd just been in and the adrenalin was pumping again. That was it, I was back into the routine and loved it. I'd had my fix and wanted more.

Throughout the twenty odd years I ran with the Boro mob I saw so many lads come and go. In the Eighties we had one of the gamest mobs in the country. Don't get me wrong, I'm not saying that we didn't have a top mob in the Nineties, because we did, but the Eighties lads were different. They were all brought up together on the same rough estates and knew each other personally. Sadly, some of them are now either dead or doing very long jail sentences, and some just drifted away from the football scene.

Some of the Eighties lads are still going to this day but not the hardcore mob we had back then. A lot of lads calmed down a bit when the police did all the dawn raids up and down the country and were jailing people indiscriminately. A lot of our lads are also now banned from the games and, if I'm honest, it seems to be working. Lads who never went in the Eighties, simply because they were too young, missed so much. Things were so different then and we got away with a lot more than you can now. Nowadays you can attend matches for months without a single off, but back then it was every single week. It didn't matter where you went, it was week in and week out. A lot of clubs now have lads who just

221

turn up in their Stone Island gear and strut about trying to get noticed, and would probably shit themselves if confronted. In the early days we all wore the designer gear but it was the violence that was first and foremost. It was quite brutal at times but that was all part of it.

At the very first match I attended I got such a buzz from seeing the violence, I was hooked immediately. It was an addiction that lasted over two decades. Do I miss it? I miss the Eighties scene, it was something else. Nowadays it's not the same. The theory is the same but technology over the years has changed. Would I ever go back? Well, a lengthy ban when this book is published will see to it that I don't, but the things I've witnessed and the feelings I experienced over the years will always be etched into my memory. They can ban me but they can never take away those memories.

What now? I can't really see into the future; my balls aren't crystal so who knows? These days I keep myself to myself and try and do my best for the two people that matter most to me; my son, Tommy and my partner, Elaine. I work hard now; have a nice house, and a lovely family, so life is sweet at the moment.

I'll probably get some good reports for writing this book but I will also get some shit as well. Either way I'm not arsed. It was how I saw things through my eyes. People might have seen things differently. No two people's minds are the same and opinions vary. All I can say is you're entitled to your own opinion, as I am mine. Anyone who thinks what I've written is shite, then all I can say is stop criticising it, get off your lazy lard-arse, spend month after month researching and writing, and write your own fucking book.

To those of you who have enjoyed what I have written, thank you for taking the time to read it. I hope you can relate to it in some shape or form and hope it brings back some good memories.

I just want to remind you of that wicked adrenalin feeling you get when you first walk out of someone's train station knowing they are waiting for you; a mixture of anticipation, fear, excitement and aggression, all rolled into one. If you're a true lad and know the score then you will agree. It's what made us tick. And as Arnold once said, "I'll be back!"

I'm still close to some of the active lads and some that used to be active. I've shared some brilliant days with them and without them this book could not have been written. So fair play to everyone who I've ever been associated with over the years.

You've all probably noticed by now that I've mentioned very few names, not even aliases or nicknames, for obvious reasons. I hope the book has met everybody's expectations and that I've represented our mob well. You certainly brightened up my Saturday afternoons. Also, if anybody who reads this book has ever had the misfortune of taking a whack from me, then you were either in the wrong place at the wrong time or you deserved it. Either way, learn to duck next time!

Catch ya later!

ACKNOWLEDGEMENTS

A special acknowledgment goes to a special friend who is no longer with us, Paul "Gunner" Easton.

Gunner, you were always there for me through the many years we worked together on the doors. Although you were small in stature, you had a heart as big as a Lion's.

You know you were always the one I'd have by my side in any situation because I knew when everyone around was losing their head, you'd be there for me to back me up 100 per cent. The times we shared over the years are now etched in my memory. We had some proper laughs together, and it was a great loss when you passed away.

You will never be forgotten, and I hope one day we'll meet up again somewhere and laugh about the times we shared. You never know, mate, we might even get a job together working Heaven's door – although it will probably be the other door, down below, that we'll work. We'd have a better laugh down there, anyway!

RIP GUNNER, NEVER FORGOTTEN.

* * *

THE BRICK

This acknowledgement is to my partner, Elaine.

Elaine, when we met some years ago, I had just come out of a very bad time in my life and I suppose at the time I was unpredictable.

You stood by me and gave me the love and happiness I had longed for. You are everything I could ever ask for – beautiful, a body to die for, and a wicked sense of humour. We have shared some funny and happy times together and over the years have become best friends and soul mates.

With your love and support, Elaine, you have made me the person I am today, and I thank you for that. You are my rock, Elaine, and as you already know I love you to bits and hope we can share many, many years of happiness together.

I will be there for you always, through thick and thin, and I just want to say thank you for guiding me in the right direction. But most of all, thank you just for being you. XXX

* * *

A big thank you to my future mother-in-law, Margaret, for doing all the work on the computer to make this book possible. I couldn't have done it without you.

Also anybody who contributed to this book, whether it be with input, photos or just ideas, it all came together in the end, so cheers lads, I owe you one.

A big shout also to all the match lads, new and old. All the Hemlington lads, Acklam lads, Linthorpe lads, the PEC, Stockton lads, Redcar lads, lads from the Brunton Arms, and anybody I've ever been involved with over the years, especially all the doormen from Wicker's World, Blaise's, Madison, Flares and Gilzean's. The laughs we shared are priceless.

Also, by writing this book I will probably get called violent, a drug taker, thief, thug, and so on. For fuck's sake, change the record. It's all been said before. If you can come up with some new names for me I would be more than happy to hear them.

Regards,

The Brick.

To whom it may concern and the powers that be:

Everything you read in this book is pure nonsense, bull, lies, call it what you want. I am just a normal lad with an over-active imagination. And as for Kit Kat the cat, I didn't really strangle it. I was choked myself when I learned of his death.